For or Better or for Worse

Lessons From Old Testament Couples

Gordon E. Christo

Pacific Press® Publishing Association
Nampa, Idaho
Oshawa, Ontario, Canada
www.pacificpress.com

Designed by Dennis Ferree
Cover illustration © Justinen Creative Group

Copyright 2007 by
Pacific Press® Publishing Association
Printed in the United States of America
All rights reserved

Unless otherwise noted, Scripture quotations are from the NIV, the HOLY BIBLE, NEW INTERNATIONAL VERSION, copyright © 1973, 1978, 1984 International Bible Society. Used by permission of Zondervan Bible Publishers.
Scriptures quoted from NKJV are from the Holy Bible, The New King James Version, copyright © 1979, 1980, 1982 by Thomas Nelson, Inc. Used by permission.

Additional copies of this book are available
by calling toll free 1-800-765-6955 or
by visiting http://www.adventistbookcenter.com.

ISBN 13: 978-0-8163-2197-1
ISBN 10: 0-8163-2197-3

07 08 09 10 • 5 4 3 2 1

Dedication

Lovingly dedicated to Rosenita, my inspiration.

Table of Contents

1. Idyllic Love: Adam and Eve 9
2. Obedient Love: Abraham and Sarah 18
3. Silent Love: Isaac and Rebekah 27
4. Ardent Love: Jacob and Rachel 38
5. Supportive Love: Moses and Zipporah 48
6. Stupid Love: Samson and Delilah 56
7. Selfless Love: Boaz and Ruth 65
8. Tender Love: Elkanah and Hannah 74
9. Steadfast Love: The Jobs 84
10. Selfish Love: David and Bathsheba 93
11. Domineering Love: Ahab and Jezebel 103
12. Forgiving Love: Hosea and Gomer 112
13. Jealous Love: Yahweh and Israel 121

Preface

God is love, and He created us in His image to love. Our highest priority is to love—both God and fellow human beings. So when we love, we are fulfilling God's purpose for us. But what do we mean by the word *love*? Many kinds of love are exhibited in the Old Testament—some admirable and some dishonorable. All have at times been translated "love," but actually have a variety of meanings.

The most common Hebrew word for love is *'âhab*. This word describes most types of affection. It is used to designate God's feelings toward us, as well as our love for other persons, food, or various objects. Between persons, *'âhab* signifies more than just a romantic feeling; it signifies the entire relationship.

Another word, *'âgab*, is usually translated "lust" and is used in the Bible mostly by Ezekiel to describe Israel's running after Assyria against God's instructions. As the prophet put it, they " 'lusted after [their] lovers, the Assyrians' " (Ezekiel 23:5).

A third word for love is *râchâm*, derived from the word for *womb*, which naturally has the connotation of compassion and is often used to describe a mother's love for her children. But men, too, can demonstrate this caring attitude for others. Hosea's child is named *Lo Ruhamah*, which means "not loved" or "not pitied." Later the name was adjusted to "loved."

Preface

Yet another word for love, *dôwd*, denotes passionate love. Related to the word for *breast* (Proverbs 5:19), it is the word used in the Proverbs for "drink[ing] deep of *love*" (7:18, italics added), and in the Song of Solomon for the *love* that is better than wine (Song of Solomon 1:2, 4). The Shulamite called Solomon *dodi*, which means "my lover."

Finally, there is *châshaq*. The root word for this means "clasp," or "attachment," such as a clamp that was used in construction. By extension the word refers to a "yearning for," or "desire to be attached to." Hamor, the prince of Shechem, felt this when he saw Dinah, the daughter of Jacob. He was drawn to her and loved her (Genesis 34:3).

Many other shades of love are revealed by couples mentioned in the Bible. The love stories in this book focus on one aspect for each couple, but most relationships had multiple facets that included (or excluded) respect, trust, kinship, devotion, loyalty, support, and generosity.

CHAPTER 1

Idyllic Love: Adam and Eve

Before God created human beings, He prepared a beautiful home for them. Every part of the earth was a paradise. Shrubs and trees draped with flowers, fruit, and vines were arranged in a landscaped garden. Rivers, streams, and lakes refreshed everything. Fleecy clouds curtained the blue sky. No ugly stones, no thorns or thistles, absolutely nothing tarnished the scene.

But God made one corner of the earth breathtakingly beautiful. Four tributaries flowed into a river that watered the trees, shrubs, and colorful flowering plants. Birds of the brightest hues filled the air with cheerful tunes. The seas, too, had their share of splashes of color, perhaps like the coral reefs we see today. In this paradise, every bird was friendly, every animal was tame, and the reptiles were the most beautiful. And all the birds and animals lived together in harmony.

This was the setting God arranged for the first couple. Nothing in the Garden detracted from their joy. They had no bills to pay and no shortage of food. The two could spend all their time together, and their joy could last forever and ever.

Help needed

Have you ever been to the zoo all alone? If so, you can begin to imagine Adam's life before Eve was created. But instead of having to walk from cage to cage to see the animals, the creatures came parading right in front of him. Also, instead of having to look at a sign telling what animal it was, Adam was assigned to name them himself, and he did—whatever came to his mind as he saw them. They came waddling, scampering, trotting, crawling, flying, gliding, or swimming.

Even if Adam did not assign feminine forms of the names, such as lioness, cow, doe, hen, etc., he must have noticed that each animal had a counterpart. Each romped and played with a partner.[1] He thoroughly enjoyed the variety of animals, and their antics entertained him; but Adam wanted to share the joy with someone. Maybe there were more creatures somewhere, perhaps even one he could communicate with. But the more animal pairs Adam saw, the more he realized that he was alone and lonely. And so God declared that only one thing in His creation was not good: " 'It is not good for the man to be alone. I will make a helper for him' " (Genesis 2:18).

Adam lay down and gave in to the heavy drowsiness that overwhelmed him. And when he awoke, a beautiful creature gazed down at him, making him feel shy. Instinctively Adam knew he had found his mate. The common English versions render his response as " 'This is now . . .' " (Genesis 2:23). But a better translation would be "*Now this one is . . .*," or "At last I've found one . . ."

The emotion that overcame Adam included not only attraction but also relief. Finally there was a creature with whom he could identify. Having been fashioned from one of Adam's ribs, she was the part of him that was missing. The previous loneliness had disappeared.

God referred to this new creature as a "helper" for Adam. A helper or assistant is often viewed as less important than the person being assisted. But the Hebrew word for *helper* is usually used in a spiritual sense to refer to God (Psalms 46:5; 79:9; 121:2). It is also used in a military sense for an allied country, usually a superpower (Ezekiel 30:8; Isaiah 31:1–3).[2] Normally when we call for help, we desire assistance from a stronger person, though anyone might do. So we see that the reference to Eve as a helper does not necessarily indicate that her role was less important than Adam's.

Idyllic Love: Adam and Eve

God announced that He was going to create a helper to be Adam's "opposite." Some versions render it "corresponding," or "suitable." The Hebrew term suggests a counterpart or complement for him. Eve was to be neither Adam's superior rescuer nor his inferior assistant. Both of them were to complement each other as opposites. Both were to combine their efforts for a common cause.

United they stand

The Bible writer added this comment to the Creation story: "For this reason a man will leave his father and mother and be united to his wife, and they will become one flesh" (Genesis 2:24).

Adam and Eve were to be *one* in ways that animal pairs would never be. Eve belonged to Adam because she was taken out from him. The Hebrew for woman, *'ishah*, is derived from the word for man, *'ish*.[3] Eve's creation was special, unlike that of all the other animal pairs.

God referred to Eve as Adam's helper, but Adam couldn't help waxing poetic. He called Eve " 'bone of my bones / and flesh of my flesh' " (Genesis 2:23). "Flesh and bones" is better translated "blood" in English and signifies close genetic kinship as in "blood relatives." Laban used the expression "flesh and blood" for Jacob, his nephew (Genesis 29:14). Abimelech addressed his half brothers using the same idiom (Judges 9:2), which could denote even being members of the same tribe (2 Samuel 5:1; 19:12–14). In the story of Job, Satan asserted that if Job's "flesh and bones" were touched, Job would curse God (Job 2:4). This did not happen when Job's literal flesh and bones were afflicted, but it is interesting to note that the temptation to curse God came from Job's wife—his figurative flesh and bones.

Eve was almost a clone of Adam, sharing the same genetic content. However, as a female, Eve was not a real clone of Adam. Adam's expression perhaps sums it up best: Eve was his kin as close as you can get, bone of his bones and flesh of his flesh. The relationship between spouses is usually considered the closest—closer than parent-child, and closer than siblings.

It is not Adam but the narrator who observed that therefore all men must leave their parents and join to their spouses. Of course,

Adam had no earthly parents to leave, but the narrator was stating the model for future marriages. Some of the most important men in Hebrew history, such as Moses and Jacob, actually joined their wives' families; but they were exceptions. Early Hebrews were "patrilocal," joining the family of the husband. In later Hebrew society, the couple set up their own home, separate from both their parents' homes, forming a new unit.

Jesus, commenting on the creation of Adam and Eve and the uniting of the two into one, told the Pharisees, " 'What God has joined together, let man not separate' " (Matthew 19:6). Husbands and wives were not to be identical in thought and function, for that would be duplication of effort. Just as in the Godhead, there was to be no discord; but they were to be united in nature, thought, and purpose. Before they sinned, Adam and Eve lived in complete unity.

One in God's image

The "two being one" constituted one aspect of the image in man of God, who is Three in One. When God made man in His image, the author qualified it with the phrase "male and female" (Genesis 1:27). Male and female combine to reflect God's image. One gender alone cannot mirror God. Men and women were programmed to seek and combine with the other for the continuation of the human race.

Associating God with the masculine gender alone limits God. God has qualities that the feminine represents as well. Though the Hebrew word for *God* is formed with the masculine plural ending, the Hebrew word for *Holy Spirit* is feminine in form. The Old Testament depicts God as a hen with chicks and, significantly, the fruit of the Holy Spirit are those qualities that women find easier to exhibit: kindness, goodness, faithfulness, gentleness, self-control, etc. Neither gender by itself can adequately represent God.

Adam and Eve were created in God's physical image. The Hebrew word for *image* is also used for a statue, a physical likeness. When God said, " 'Let us make man in our image,' " He qualified it by adding " 'in our likeness' " (Genesis 1:26). The same comparison

Idyllic Love: Adam and Eve

is used in describing Seth's likeness to Adam (Genesis 5:3). Seth resembled his dad.

The image of God also refers to the dominion of humans over all creation. When God purposed to create man in His image and likeness, He added, " 'let them rule over . . .' " (Genesis 1:26). Adam and Eve were, and all humans are, God's governors on this earth, and in that sense, too, we reflect God.

God had said, "Let *us* make man in *our* image." God is plural, and so is man. God is love and cannot be so if singular. So also the man and woman are meant to love and be loved, to reflect God's image in a social sense. The intent that male and female are collectively labeled "man" is borne out clearly in the following text: "When God created man, he made him in the likeness of God. He created them male and female and blessed them. And when they were created, he called them 'man' " (Genesis 5:1, 2).

Divided they fall

Traditionally, we have been taught that Eve succumbed to temptation because she had wandered off alone in the Garden. But some believe that Adam was with her. They quote Genesis 3:6, "she took some and ate it. She also gave some to her husband, who was with her, and he ate it."

The Hebrew has several words that may be translated "with." Two important ones are *'êtsel* and *'im*. The latter is used in this passage. *Esel* is the preposition that is used to denote location beside. (See Genesis 39:14, 18.) By contrast *im* denotes relationship. "Immanuel" in Isaiah 7:14; 8:8, 10, begins with the preposition *im* and means "God with us." It indicates a relational, not a geographical, position. Genesis 3:6, therefore, does not strictly demand that we see Adam positioned beside Eve when she is tempted. Adam used the same preposition in 3:12 to remind God about the woman He had put with him. It is a relational *with*.

"The points to be emphasized (for *im*) are (1) the basic conception conveyed is that of fellowship, companionship, common experiences of suffering, prosperity etc.; (2) the term can emphasize a common lot regardless of social status, location, etc.; (3) the term, as in all other prepositions, may have definite theological implications."[4]

If Adam had been present with Eve, we should have to answer several questions: (1) Why did the serpent address only Eve? Surely the snake would not have taken the risk of ignoring the man, who could have interfered. (2) Why did Adam stay quiet during the encounter? It would be strange for him not to intervene. (3) Why did God not condemn Adam for listening to the serpent, but condemned him only for listening to his wife? Obviously Adam had not listened to the serpent.

If, on the other hand, Adam was absent, he should have asked Eve for some details as to how she acquired the forbidden fruit, what she was doing with it, and how it tasted, etc. Instead, he just took it and ate it.

We may surmise that Adam understood enough about Eve's taking the fruit that he also understood its implications for her. He then had to make the decision whether to join Eve in her lot or let her suffer alone.

The difference

Eve had not previously experienced deception and lies. Throughout practically all of Eden, Adam and Eve could trust anything without being on guard. Satan was not allowed to follow them around the Garden, constantly trying to trap them. He had access to them only if they ventured close to the forbidden tree. But in the center of the Garden, in the vicinity of that tree, they should have been extremely alert because he was waiting there.

Satan dared not appear in his real form and give himself away. He would have to select a medium that would arouse the greatest interest and the least suspicion. He chose the serpent. He didn't present himself as a rival of God, but pretended to be one of His creatures. Eve had forgotten exactly what God had said and thought He said they would die if they so much as touched the fruit, rather than die if they ate it (Genesis 3:4). She noticed that the serpent was touching the fruit and not dying, thus seeming to validate his argument. She believed Satan's lie, and before she knew what was happening, she was eating the fruit.

Idyllic Love: Adam and Eve

The apostle Paul agreed that Eve, sincere and devoted to God, was deceived: "But I am afraid that just as Eve was deceived by the serpent's cunning, your minds may somehow be led astray from your sincere and pure devotion to Christ" (2 Corinthians 11:3).

Adam's case was different. The devil was not present in person where Eve met Adam, and he could not yet speak to humans except near the tree. But Eve was now the devil's agent. Adam was not deceived. He realized that Eve had been taken in by the devil; it was too late for her. They had not yet witnessed death, but he knew that something awful would happen to her. He himself would be safe if he didn't eat the fruit, but he could not bear the thought of losing his wife. Eve was so much a part of Adam that he thought that he could not bear to be apart from her. When Eve handed him the fruit and urged him to eat it, he did so, knowing full well there would be consequences.

The result

Genesis 2:25, which tells us that the couple though naked was unashamed, not only closes the Creation story but actually introduces the story of the Fall. The Hebrew word for "naked" is 'ârôm. But it is practically identical to the word for "shrewd," which is also 'ârôm. The next chapter, the story of the Fall in Genesis 3, begins with the statement that the serpent was "more cunning" ('ârôm) than all the other creatures (NKJV).

Adam and Eve, who previously had no shame at their lack of clothing, suddenly felt exposed and ashamed. That this was a physical nakedness is immediately apparent because they had sewed fig leaves for themselves (Genesis 3:7). They were ashamed of themselves and shy because of the presence of the other.

However, another form of nakedness also becomes obvious. The animal-skin garment that God made for them did more than cover physical nakedness. It also pointed to a provision to cover their spiritual nakedness. They now felt shame in God's presence about their sinful hearts. God, however, made provision for that too at the same time. Adam and Eve would not have to run away from God ashamed because of their sin.

Adam and Eve, whose relation had been one of joy and harmony, suddenly became selfish. Adam fired the first salvo by blaming Eve for his fall. Although he had purposefully consumed the fruit to share in the tragic lot of the woman, now at the first opportunity to defend her, he accused her instead. True, the finger-pointing was only indirect; directly, he was accusing God for providing him with an agent of temptation.

Exposed, Eve fell back on the same trick and blamed the serpent.

The consequences

In one stroke Adam and Eve lost everything—innocence, dominion, immortality, Edenic home, and security. In their place, they acquired guilt, competition with beasts, death, expulsion, fear, struggle for existence, etc.

A couple in a perfectly harmonious love relationship can bear all kinds of hardship as long as they still have each other, but in addition to all these losses, Adam and Eve lost their idyllic relationship.

God now told Eve, " 'Your desire will be for your husband, / and he will rule over you' " (Genesis 3:16). Adam would develop a tendency to dominate her, and this would mar their relationship. God foresaw that some men would distort their leadership role into subjugation by force. God did not decree such subjugation but foretold what would be as a consequence of Eve's sin. This was contrary to the original intention of God for husband-wife relationships.

God also predicted that women would permit this dominance because of a natural desire for their husbands and for children. Males would take advantage of this desire.

The Bible considers it to be the correct attitude for a woman to submit herself to her husband (1 Peter 3:1). Some have attempted to limit this subordination by pointing out that the woman was to submit only to her husband and not to men in general. Others have used the illustration of Sarah obeying Abraham and calling him "master" and provide it as an example of true subordination.

Yet, wives are told not to give way to fear (verse 6). They may win over their husbands with their behavior, rather than by words

Idyllic Love: Adam and Eve

(verse 1). A woman's quiet and gentle spirit, which makes her beautiful (verse 4), can often work wonders in helping her get her way.

Peter's advice includes protection for the woman as well. He instructs husbands to treat their wives with respect because they are the weaker partners (verse 7). The stronger partner is not to take advantage of the weaker. Peter indicates that neglecting to do this "will hinder your prayers" (verse 7). In other words, a husband's mistreatment of his wife could prevent his prayers from being answered.

༄

The subordination of wives was not part of God's original plan but was introduced after the Fall. Whereas Adam and Eve lived in complete harmony earlier, now they would have differences of opinion. In a sinful world, two equals would not be able to live in absolute agreement. In order to maintain peace at home, one would have to give in. This is not fair, but so are many other aspects of life. One day, however, justice will be restored, and in the earth made new, relationships will again be idyllic.

---

1. While the text does not say that God created animals male and female, He did command the fish and the fowl to be fruitful and multiply. The similar command at the end of the sixth day presumably applied not only to the humans but to all that was created that day, including animals.

2. The Ugaritic equivalent means "to rescue." See Carl Shulz, "*ezer*," *Theological Wordbook of the Old Testament* II, 660.

3. Another Hebrew word for man is *Adam*, taken from the Hebrew word for ground, *Adamah*.

4. Gerard Van Groningen, "*esel*," *Theological Wordbook of the Old Testament* II, 677.

CHAPTER 2

Obedient Love: Abraham and Sarah

The story of Abraham and Sarah picks up where the story of Adam and Eve ended—the loss of equality for women. As a result of Eve's sin, God had predicted that men would "rule" over their wives (Genesis 3:16). Sarah is now uplifted as the representative of this new model— one who submits to her husband. The apostle Peter praised Sarah for obeying Abraham and calling him "lord."[1] "In this manner, in former times, the holy women who trusted in God also adorned themselves, being submissive to their own husbands, as Sarah obeyed Abraham, calling him lord, whose daughters you are if you do good and are not afraid with any terror" (1 Peter 3:5, 6, NKJV).

The Hebrew word for "husband" is *ba'al*, which literally means "lord." Baal, the local god, was considered by the Canaanites as lord of the land. Instead, the Israelites were to acknowledge Yahweh as *the* Lord of the land and Lord of their lives. In the home, however, the husband was to be lord. Peter commended Sarah for showing the way. But Peter also cautioned husbands not to take advantage of being the stronger partner, but to treat their wives with respect and consideration. Peter's principle is for harmony in the home. To maintain peace, one should be submissive, while the other ought to be considerate and respectful.

Also, it was not that wives were never, ever to get their way. Peter says the ideal wife would win her husband over not by words but by

Obedient Love: Abraham and Sarah

her behavior—the purity and reverence of her life. Peter adds that women of faith made themselves beautiful before God by their gentle and quiet spirit rather than by outward show. Sarah was legendary not only for her physical beauty but for her inner beauty demonstrated by submission to her husband. Peter upheld this as a model for all wives.

Leaving home with husband

Hebrews 11 praises Abraham for his great faith first demonstrated in his leaving his homeland and striking out as God directed, living as a nomad seeking the City of God. Hebrews 11 does not commend Sarah for faith. It is not Abraham's type of faith that caused her to leave with him but willingness to follow her husband wherever he went.

One can imagine the kind of conversation that could have ensued when Abraham said, "Sarah, we are to leave this place." Sarah would have been excused for responding, "Are you crazy? Why now? We are nearing the age of retirement and should be thinking of settling, not moving!" Certainly the older we get, the less willing we are to adjust to change. Leaving the security of family and friends to start life anew can be stressful at any age. Old age in Eastern culture is the time to think of going back to family from wherever one had left to make his fortune.

Next Sarah could have asked, "All right, where are we going?" When Abraham responded, "I am not sure," Sarah could again be forgiven if she turned incredulous. "You don't know! Where do we go if we don't know where to go?" And when Abraham said, "God will show us the place," Sarah could easily have responded, "What if we don't like it there? Wouldn't it be nice to know where we're going?" Deciding what to take and what to leave behind is so much easier when we know where we are going. How many wives would be willing to follow their husbands knowing that even they don't know where they are heading?

One thing seemed certain: They were leaving behind city life and heading for rural living. Abraham asked Sarah to give up the comforts of civilization—a solid home, running water, a private bath, shopping markets. Living in a tent may have its attractions for a vacation—but to live that way for the rest of one's life? It's difficult to imagine most wives not offering some kind of resistance.

So Sarah's willingness to follow Abraham must be commended. She has asked no questions and made no comments worth recording.

Sacrificing her interests for his

The only times Sarah is recorded as taking the initiative was in suggesting a way for God's promise of an heir to be fulfilled and then in solving the problem that her first suggestion created. God had promised Abraham, " 'I will make you into a great nation / and I will bless you' " (Genesis 12:2). This promise was not fulfilled within what seemed to them a reasonable time, and Abraham and his wife grew quite old. As they aged, the lack of an heir became more serious.

Abraham had earlier suggested to God that he and Sarah adopt their servant Eliezer (Genesis 15:3). Eliezer was likely the chief servant to whom Abraham entrusted all that he owned and whom he sent to negotiate a wife for Isaac (Genesis 24). Some ancient Nuzi tablets[2] shed light on the custom of a childless couple adopting a servant or the servant's son to inherit property. In return, the adopted servant agreed to ensure the adoptive parents a decent burial. The contract stated, however, that it would be invalidated if the couple subsequently had their own child. Abraham was within his legal rights to think of such a solution, an accepted custom of the time.

However, God did not have an adopted son in mind. The heir would be Abraham's biological son. God insisted, " 'This man will not be your heir, but a son coming from your own body will be your heir' " (Genesis 15:4). Some New Testament passages declare that Abraham's seed are not his biological descendents but those who have faith (Romans 9:8; Galatians 3:7). Abraham and Sarah could do without an heir, but God needed them to have a son so that His promises could be fulfilled. Not only was the seed to be biological, as God was saying now, but the Messiah, too, was to come from the line of Abraham (Galatians 3:16).

Obedient Love: Abraham and Sarah

One suggestion to secure such a biological son originated from Sarah. After they had been in Canaan ten years, she suggested that Abraham take her maidservant, Hagar, as a second wife (Genesis 16:1–3). They had acquired many servants during their visit to Egypt (Genesis 12:16), and Hagar could have been one of them. Again, some Nuzi tablets have parallels. The wife of a childless couple could give her slave girl to her husband, retaining authority over any children that might result from the union. The Nuzi contracts also state that the son borne by a slave girl would inherit all the property unless the legal wife bore a son later. A son born thus to Abraham would fulfill God's promise of an heir "coming from [Abraham's] body."

This would not have been an easy offer for Sarah to make. She must have considered the matter deeply before coming up with the suggestion. The heir would be Abraham's seed, but not hers. It meant that she was prepared to be excluded from God's promises to Abraham for his sake. This was a tremendous sacrifice. The fact that it was she who came up with the idea rather than Abraham shows her willingness to do what was best for him regardless of the implications for herself. She was not pressured into this alternative by a competing wife who was bearing children (such as Rachel with Leah). It was just her genuine interest in her husband's fortunes.

In only a few months, Sarah realized her mistake. As soon as Hagar knew she was pregnant, she behaved arrogantly toward her mistress. Sarah complained to Abraham saying, " 'I put my servant in your arms and now that she knows she is pregnant, she despises me. May the LORD judge between you and me' " (Genesis 16:5). Abraham could have said, "Right. May He judge between you and me. Wasn't this your idea in the first place?" But instead he wisely said, " 'Do with her whatever you think best' " (Genesis 16:6). Sarah didn't expel Hagar but made her life so miserable that Hagar ran away. Hagar then complained to God, who instructed her to return and submit to her mistress, Sarah (Genesis 16:9). Thus peace was maintained in the camp.

Paul further adds that those who attempt to gain salvation by works are in spiritual bondage and tend to persecute those who rely on faith and grace for their salvation, and who are free (Galatians

4:23, 29). The symbolism is appropriate because the attempt to use the slave Hagar produced a son in the natural way, whereas the free Sarah acquired a son by faith.

Sarah's human attempt to solve God's "problem" resulted in several other problems. Hagar disturbed Sarah's peace by her words and actions after becoming pregnant. Hagar's attitude brought stress to Abraham and Sarah's relationship. And as Ishmael grew, he posed a threat to Isaac, who naturally displaced him. Abraham and Sarah lost a servant—first when Hagar ran away and again when they sent her away. The descendants of Ishmael continued to be at odds with the descendants of Isaac through the centuries.

Endangering herself for his sake

Though Abraham and Sarah were both children of Terah, they did not share the same mother. When God called Abraham to leave home, one of Abraham's concerns in facing the unknown was related to his beautiful wife and half sister. Abraham feared that the heathen people he would live among would kill him so they could have Sarah. He thought of a simple solution. He requested of her, " ' "This is how you can show your love to me: Everywhere we go, say of me, 'He is my brother' " ' " (Genesis 20:13).

In effect, what Abraham is telling Sarah is "If you love me, you will tell a lie." She could easily have retorted, "If you love me, you will not ask me to take this risk." But Abraham convinced Sarah that if the truth of their relationship were known, he would be killed and Sarah taken anyway. This way, at least his life would be spared.

We have no way of knowing how many times they used this bluff. We do know that it backfired twice. The first time was in Egypt. The second was in Gerar. Even in her old age Sarah was lovely to behold. On both occasions, it was the king of the land who, learning of her beauty and being told she was Abraham's sister, took Sarah to his palace to marry. Explaining the matter to God, who held the whole household ransom (Genesis 12:17; 20:18), Pharaoh only accused Abraham (not Sarah) of lying (Genesis 12:19). But King Abimelech reported that not only had Abraham claimed that Sarah was his sister, but that Sarah, too, had said, " ' "He is my brother" ' " (Genesis 20:5).

Obedient Love: Abraham and Sarah

It is difficult to imagine how Abraham had hoped to get out of possible difficulties. Possibly as her "brother," he hoped to put off marriage plans. Perhaps Abraham had such faith in God that he expected Him to take care of any problem that might ensue. However, it looks more like a demonstration of lack of faith in God. At any rate, Abraham seems to have been worried primarily about his own safety. He expressed no concern for Sarah's security.

Sarah could have responded, "What about me? What am I supposed to do as the wife of the king?" But again the dutiful wife was to be subservient to the wishes and well-being of her husband. The next time Abraham instructed her to repeat the lie again, Sarah could have said, "I'm afraid. Remember what happened last time? Why do I get to take all the risks and you get all the gifts and grand treatment?"

Fortunately, both times God intervened to tell the truth to the heathen kings. Also, fortunately, Egyptian and Canaanite ethics were superior to Abraham's in this regard, and Sarah was spared.

Laughter in the home

Though Abimelech, king of Gerar, had taken Sarah innocently, believing her to be the sister of Abraham, still God had closed up the wombs of all the women in the king's household. Ironically, it turned out that Abraham, the man who himself had no offspring and whose wife was barren, mediated for the house of Abimelech so that their women could again bear children. "Then Abraham prayed to God, and God healed Abimelech, his wife and his slave girls so they could have children again, for the LORD had closed up every womb in Abimelech's household because of Abraham's wife Sarah" (Genesis 20:17, 18).

Sarah believed that the Lord had prevented her from having children. Fourteen years after Ishmael's birth, Sarah was eighty-nine years old. The patriarchs near Abraham's time had their first son between ages thirty and thirty-five. Terah was born when Nahor, his father (with the same name as Terah's son), was twenty-nine. By comparison, when God first promised them a son, Abraham and Sarah were more than double the age at which they could have expected their first child. By the time the latest assurance came, they were three times the average age for a first child.

Abraham lived to the age of 175 (Genesis 25:7). Sarah died at 127 (Genesis 23:1). Their son Isaac lived to be 180 years old (Genesis 35:28). Proportionately, it could be today as though Abraham and Sarah were in their fifties. Many years had passed since God made the first promise. Obviously, the older they became, the less likely it seemed that the promised child would be born.

But God returned when Abraham was ninety-nine years old, twenty-four years after He first made the covenant with Abraham, and God again promised to multiply Abraham's seed. Not surprisingly, Abraham thought it was a joke. The record says, "Abraham fell facedown; he laughed and said to himself, 'Will a son be born to a man a hundred years old? Will Sarah bear a child at the age of ninety?' " (Genesis 17:17).

A short while later, three heavenly visitors came to Abraham, and while they ate the meal Sarah prepared, one of them predicted that the promised child would be born in about a year (Genesis 18:10). Like typical Bedouin women, Sarah had stayed out of sight but not out of hearing. Just behind the entrance to the tent, she laughed to herself when she heard the prediction (Genesis 18:12). This was not laughter of joy, but laughter of unbelief.

Surprisingly, God did not condemn Abraham when he laughed. But when Sarah laughed, the Lord questioned Abraham saying, " 'Why did Sarah laugh and say, "Will I really have a child, now that I am old?" ' " (Genesis 18:13). Perhaps the difference is that Sarah became afraid when questioned and denied laughing. Sarah maintained, "I did not laugh," and God insisted, "Yes, you did laugh." Whatever the reason, she tried to cover her disbelief with a lie, and the conversation ended on an uncomfortable note.

During the interval of time between Abraham's and Sarah's laughter at God's repeated promise, God told them to name the son who would be born *Isaac*, which means "he laughs" (Genesis 17:19). The word *Yitzhak* means what it sounds like—a loud, explosive laugh. When the child was finally born and named, Sarah added, " 'God has brought me laughter, and everyone who hears about this will laugh with me' " (Genesis 21:6).

Obedient Love: Abraham and Sarah

Ironically, when Isaac was weaned at about age three, Ishmael thought it was his turn to laugh. The festive occasion honoring Isaac sidelined Ishmael. The Hebrew word for Ishmael's laugh, *metzahek*, denotes derision. Hearing that laugh, Sarah sensed Ishmael's presence as a threat and insisted that the slave mother and son be dismissed. God concurred (Genesis 21:12), and Abraham wisely deferred to Sarah's request.

Sacrificing the son

Years later, when God tested Abraham by instructing him to sacrifice his son Isaac, there is no record that Abraham shared this information with Sarah. Perhaps he knew his wife well and feared that the woman who had faithfully cooperated with all of God's and Abraham's plans would oppose this one.

Sarah's faith apparently was not as strong as Abraham's. The book of Hebrews commends Abraham for his faith in being willing to offer Isaac as a sacrifice, though it describes Abraham as reasoning that God could raise Isaac from the dead (Hebrews 11:17–19). James uses Abraham as an example of both faith and works. He goes on to say that a person is justified by what he *does* in response to his faith (James 2:24). Abraham was considered righteous for what he did when he offered Isaac on the altar (James 2:21). Sarah may have lacked the faith to carry out an actual sacrifice of her child.

Canaanites had practiced child sacrifice for centuries. Molech and Chemosh, the national gods of the Ammonites and the Moabites, required that children be offered to them in a fire. Assyrians around 800 B.C. offered children to the god Addramelech. Mesha, king of Moab, offered his heir to the throne when he faced defeat in battle (2 Kings 3:27).

Abraham could well have been smugly confident that his God would never require him to do what his pagan neighbors did in their devotion to false gods. (God later instructed the Israelites, " ' "Do not give any of your children to be sacrificed to Molech, for you must not profane the name of your God" ' " [Leviticus 18:21].) Abraham's son was *the* gift from God. Imagine Abraham's shock when God actually instructed him to sacrifice his son. However, Abraham knew the voice of God and trusted Him.

In fact, he assured his servants, " 'we will come back to you' " (Genesis 22:5), reasoning that God could raise Isaac from the dead (Hebrews 11:19).

We must not pass judgment on Sarah's faith just because she is left out of the story. Obviously, the test was of Abraham's faith only. Abraham possibly struggled sufficiently over obeying God's command, and informing Sarah would have only made it harder for him.

The blessings that God gave Abraham after he passed the test included Sarah. (1) Their descendents would become numerous; (2) their descendants would take possession of the land; and (3) through their offspring, all nations of the earth would be blessed.

If Abraham is characterized by faith, Sarah is a model of trust—trust in her husband and trust in God. Peter praises her as one who did not give way to fear. That was possible only because she trusted her husband completely. On that foundation of trust, she could follow him anywhere.

---

1. For the connection between Eve and Sarah I am indebted to Richard L. Strauss, "Yes, My Lord—*The Story of Abraham and Sarah*" in the Living in Love: Secrets from Bible Marriages series, http://www.bible.org/page.php?page_id=1289.

2. A city in the fertile crescent between the Tigris and the Euphrates, where tablets dating to before the time of the patriarchs were found to shed light on the social customs of that period.

CHAPTER 3

Silent Love: Isaac and Rebekah

Sarah had been dead three years when Abraham summoned his trusted servant, probably Eliezer of Damascus to whom he had thought to bequeath his estate (Genesis 15:2). Abraham was now a very old man, and there was no way of predicting that he would actually live another thirty-five years. The matter of Isaac's marriage had been put off for too long. He needed a wife to carry on the covenant line. A messenger had earlier reported to Abraham that Nahor, his brother, and his wife, Milcah, had been blessed with eight sons (Genesis 22:20–24). Now Abraham instructed his servant to fetch a wife for Isaac from among those relatives. Even though they kept idols in their house, a girl from that family would believe in the same God as Abraham and Isaac.

Of course, there was always the outside chance that the girl would be unwilling to accompany him back to a strange land, and Eliezer needed clear instructions on how to proceed, if that turned out to be the case. In that event, he would be released from the oath. But under no circumstances was Isaac to leave the land that God had covenanted to them.

A marriage made in heaven

Abraham picked his agent well. Eliezer was concerned that God make the actual selection. He prayed as he sat near the well as the girls of the town approached to collect water for their families: " 'May it be that when I say to a girl, "Please let down your jar that I may have a drink," and she says, "Drink, and I'll water your camels too"—let her be the one you have chosen for your servant Isaac' " (Genesis 24:14).

The test Eliezer suggested was designed to help him discern God's will. It would also test the girl's character. What happened next astounded even the god-fearing servant.

A beautiful maiden approached the well. Spirited, young, and energetic, she may not have appeared the type who would accommodate an old man's request. But when he asked her for a drink, she responded pleasantly and offered to water his camels as well. And when she replied to his question that she was the granddaughter of Nahor, Eliezer was amazed.

In selecting whom to approach first, Eliezer could not have known character or past history. He judged as anyone would for the first time—outward appearance. Rebekah, he had noted, was very beautiful to look at. She was obviously charming. Her response to his request for water confirmed that she was also kind and friendly. Her offer to do more than asked revealed her to be hospitable. When he learned that she was a marriageable virgin and from the family of Nahor, he was convinced God had prospered his mission. God had led him to a fantastic young woman from the right family for his master's son. God was the real Matchmaker.

Knowing that this was the young woman God had selected, Eliezer gave Rebekah the ring and bracelets he had brought. Seeing the jewelry and hearing the story, Laban rushed back to the well and fetched Abraham's servant. When the family heard the full story, they agreed saying, " 'This is from the LORD' " (Genesis 24:50).

Differences to bridge

Nobody had any doubt that God intended for Isaac and Rebekah to be married. But there were immense differences in the backgrounds of the two that might have rendered them incompatible had they both not been committed to God and His will. They had several differences to span.

Silent Love: Isaac and Rebekah

Isaac had grown up in the countryside. Where the population is sparse, people help others and are helped in return. In simple surroundings, Isaac was raised to trust people. Also, Abraham and Sarah doted on their only son. After they sent Ishmael and Hagar away, Isaac had no competition for attention. His mother showed no interest in getting him married, and he mourned after her death for three years until Rebekah came into his life. Isaac was heir to the immense wealth of Abraham and never needed to work. He had no companions his equal, and in many ways he grew up a loner—likely unaccustomed to much communication. A sober bachelor at forty when he married, he was at least ten years beyond the normal age for marriage in those days.

Rebekah, on the other hand, had grown up in the city. In urban areas, competition is more severe and survival often depends on shrewdness. Rebekah and her brother, Laban, often demonstrated their expertise in this quality. Rebekah's parents were not as wealthy as Isaac's, so she knew how to work. Her task was to fetch water for the family. She had developed the required strength and showed she could draw enough for a caravan of camels. Because Rebekah grew up in a sizable extended family, she was better adjusted to society with many friends her age and equal. Her grandmother, Milcah, daughter of Haran, was Isaac's first cousin, though Bethuel her father, son of Nahor, was also Isaac's first cousin. Rebekah likely was a vivacious teenager.

Relationship between Isaac and Rebekah

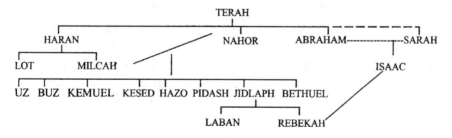

Rebekah knew what she wanted. When Eliezer saw that his mission was successful, he wanted to leave the very next day, but Rebekah's family wished for him to wait another ten days. They settled the matter by allowing Rebekah to make the decision (Genesis 24:57, 58). Until then, we have no record that anybody had bothered to consult her. She said simply, "I will go."

Rebekah's decision to go with Eliezer right away took her family by surprise. Doubtless, they hoped and expected that she would balk at leaving so quickly. However, she not only trusted in God's providence, but showed her decisiveness.

When Eliezer and Rebekah finally reached the Negev and met Isaac, Eliezer told him the entire story. Evidently, the right decision had been made. Isaac loved Rebekah, and nobody else, the remainder of his life.

Lack of communication

Isaac and Rebekah seem to have failed to bridge the age gap, the culture gap, and the temperament gap. Communication is the key to drawing people closer, but Isaac and Rebekah appear to have neglected to talk things over.

Perhaps if they had had children soon enough, raising the children would have kept them close. But for twenty years Rebekah was unable to conceive. This was all the more awkward because Abraham had by now remarried and was begetting sons at regular intervals—Zimran, Jokshan, Medan, Midian, Ishbak, and Shuah. Uncle Nahor had twelve sons, and his half brother Ishmael also had twelve sons. Isaac could have been distressed because of this. He desperately needed a son to access the covenant promises God had made to Abraham.

Isaac and Rebekah obviously loved each other. Many years later, Abimelech spotted Isaac caressing Rebekah. Showing affection is an important aspect of marriage, but much more is necessary. Husband and wife must become the closest of companions, sharing everything. Only when they know each other's minds can they cooperate to achieve the same goals. Isaac and Rebekah did not experience true companionship. They apparently did not discuss their innermost joys and concerns.

Rebekah seems to have been unable to communicate to Isaac what the Lord had told her about the elder child serving the younger. It's difficult to think she didn't try, but Isaac may have stopped really listening to her. The lack of communication in the family is evident also among the two sons. We do not read of either Jacob or Esau telling their father about the purchase of the birthright at the time of the sale or later—either before or after the blessing. Isaac did not share his plan to bless Esau with his wife, perhaps because of her fondness of Jacob. And on her part, Rebekah did not remind Isaac of God's prophecy for Jacob, but, instead, she went about devising her own plan. Even when she wanted to tell Isaac to let Jacob leave home, she could not bring herself to tell him the truth, but had to resort to a lame excuse.

Perhaps we are reading too much into what has not been recorded about their relationship, but the family definitely had a communication problem. We see a shortage of speaking out and evidence of a lack of listening.

She is my sister

When a famine struck Canaan, Isaac and Rebekah thought to move to Egypt, as Abraham had done years earlier. But God instructed them to remain in Gerar—the same place where Abraham and Sarah had their encounter with Abimelech.

There are a surprising number of similarities between Abraham's experience recorded in Genesis 20 and 21 and Isaac's recorded in Genesis 26. (1) Both took place in Gerar. (2) The name of the king in both encounters was Abimelech—though that may have been not the name but the title, because *Abimelech* means "my father is king." The person involved may have been the prince rather than the king. (3) Both Abraham and Isaac lied that their wife was their sister in order to escape being killed. (4) Both times the king found out and remonstrated with the liar. (5) On both occasions the king insisted on making a treaty. (6) Both encounters also involved disputes about wells. (7) In both instances the place was given a significant name.

The similarities are so striking that some argue that these are accounts of the same incident, but with different names. The differences however are as numerous and significant. (1) No famine is mentioned in Abraham's case. (2) There is no God-given dream to the king in Genesis 26. Abimelech discovered that Isaac and Rebekah were husband and wife when he looked out the window and saw Isaac caressing her. (3) The king in Genesis 26 did not take Rebekah to his palace. (4) No gifts were given to Isaac. (5) Abraham was not expelled from the land as Isaac was. (6) Only the women in chapter 20 were struck barren, and therefore Isaac did not have to intercede as Abraham did. (7) The herdsmen managed to retain Abraham's well. (8) No reason was given for the name of the well in chapter 21. (9) At the end of his experience, Abraham planted a tree, whereas Isaac ended the event with a feast.

Also unlike his father, Isaac did not involve his wife in planning the deception but appears to have acted on his own. He informed those who inquired that Rebekah was his sister. This was not a half-truth as in Abraham's situation. Rebekah was neither his half sister nor his cousin, though they were related. Abraham and Sarah had planned things together. Isaac and Rebekah seemed to have lacked this type of communication.

The family divide

Finally after twenty years, Isaac's prayers on behalf of Rebekah were answered, and twins were born into their family. But instead of bringing the parents closer, the presence of the boys only widened the rift between father and mother. The Bible says, "Isaac, who had a taste for wild game, loved Esau, but Rebekah loved Jacob" (Genesis 25:28).

The rivalry between Esau and Jacob began even before birth. Rebekah could feel a struggle in her womb, and God revealed that twins were struggling within her. God also foretold the rivalry that would ensue and that the younger would prevail (Genesis 25:23).

Rebekah didn't suffer a rival concubine or wife as did her mother-in-law, Sarah, and also her daughter-in-law, Rachel. But the rivalry between the sons ruined the home because it involved the husband and wife. Though the rivalry among the sons had been prophesied, it looked suspiciously as though it originated from the parents. When squabbles break out among children and the parents take sides, alienation results. Also when parents side with different children, tension develops between them as well. Isaac and Rebekah

Silent Love: Isaac and Rebekah

each supported a favorite son, and a silent battle loomed larger and larger.

Isaac loved Esau because Esau brought home wild game, which he claimed to enjoy. But one wonders why he couldn't tell the difference in the taste of a domesticated goat that Jacob brought him from wild game he expected from Esau. What Isaac may really have enjoyed was the idea of his own son excelling with the bow and arrow and bringing home game for food just as Ishmael, his older half brother, had done years before (Genesis 21:20; 27:3).

As mother, Rebekah had little appreciation for the rough outdoor life that Esau preferred. Her home was her world, and she naturally formed a bond with Jacob, who stayed by and spent time with her. Rebekah must have told Jacob about God's prophecy, that the younger would become greater. In turn, Jacob must have relished informing his mother how he had acquired the birthright from his brother for a bowl of food.

It is easy to picture Esau as the older, bigger, and stronger sibling. Yet they were twins—really exactly the same age. In the case of identical twins it is sometimes difficult to know which was first born. The Bible records a midwife tying a thread around the wrist to identify the first born (cf. Genesis 38:28–30). In Rebekah's case it was easy. The two were nowhere near identical.

Sêâr means "hairy," and the name *Esau* may be related to that word. Evidently, he was unusually hairy. He is also described as red; the word for that is *edom*, which translates as "muddy." But the Bible says the reason he was nicknamed *Edom* was that he sold his birthright for some red stew (Genesis 25:30).

Jacob means "he grasps the heel," which is what he was doing when he was born—grasping his brother's heel. But Esau interpreted that name figuratively as meaning "one who deceives."

The birthright: covenant promises

When famine again struck Canaan, Isaac planned to travel to Egypt, as his father had earlier. Egypt was watered by the Nile and not subject to annual rains. But God instructed Isaac, " 'Stay in this land for a while, and I will be with you and will bless you. For to you and your descendants I will give all these lands and will confirm the oath I swore to your father Abraham' " (Genesis 26:3).

God listed the aspects of the promises He was making to Isaac. They are identical to what was promised to Abraham: (1) His descendents would be numerous; (2) they would be given possession of the land; and (3) through his offspring all nations of the earth would be blessed.

These promises seemed far-fetched. Isaac and Rebekah had no children yet, but they were promised descendants as numerous as the stars. They were nomads wandering from place to place, but God would give them "all these lands."

Usurping the birthright

No doubt Rebekah told her favorite son, Jacob, what the Lord had told her about the elder serving the younger. Acquiring the birthright preoccupied Jacob's mind from a young age. He became obsessed with the idea, wondering how to get it. Then one day Esau, famished from an outing, returned and smelled some food stewing. When Esau begged for some food, Jacob, who was cooking, sensed his opportunity. Esau readily sold his birthright for some red lentil stew.

The sale of the birthright confirmed that Esau was disinterested in religious matters and unfit to be the spiritual leader of the clan. Jacob, on the other hand, was farsighted. He desired the spiritual leadership, was cunning enough to trick his brother out of it, and even got the transaction sealed by an oath before giving him the food.[1] Esau ate and went away unconcerned about what he had frittered away. Isaac should have been concerned about this.

Years later, Isaac decided it was time to confirm the birthright and the accompanying blessings on one of his sons, and so he called for Esau. He made no effort to conceal what he had in mind, but neither did he consult his wife about it. She heard him say to Esau, " 'Prepare me the kind of tasty food I like and bring it to me to eat, so that I may give you my blessing before I die' " (Genesis 27:4).

The aging Isaac had two things in mind. He was getting old and needed to pass on his blessing, and his mouth was watering for

Silent Love: Isaac and Rebekah

some tasty food. Here we encounter a play on words. While Esau sold his *bekôwrah* (birthright) for a bowl of lentils, Isaac will give his *berâkâh* (blessing) in exchange for some venison. But *Rebekah* will try to get the *berâkâh* for her favorite son. When she overheard the conversation between Isaac and Esau, she quickly got into action.

The family feud now came to a head. On the one side we have Isaac—old, feeble, and practically blind, a simple man who yearned to eat some tasty food and then he would bless his favorite son. On the other side we have a mother from a cunning family (any of whom would cheat their own relatives) and her son Jacob, who revealed that he had inherited some of that cunning.

Esau and Isaac were the hungry ones. Esau had earlier hungered for the aromatic lentil stew, and Isaac now yearned for the venison. Jacob and Rebekah were the cooks and took advantage of it.

When Rebekah instructed Jacob to bring two kids from their flock so she could prepare them before Esau returned, Jacob expressed no ethical objection to his mother's suggestion. His primary concern was being caught. In response to that fear, Rebekah clothed Jacob with Esau's best clothes, covered the bare parts of his arms and neck with goatskin to simulate Esau's thick body hair, and bade him, " 'Just do what I say' " (Genesis 27:13).

We could defend Rebekah. She was fighting the unjust institution of the blessing by which one child inherited everything and the other nothing (Genesis 27:37). This is especially unfair in the case of twins. Or perhaps she thought she was carrying out the will of God, who had predicted the dominance of the younger. Maybe as the mother, she knew, as Isaac must have, that Esau was unsuited for the birthright and the blessings that came with it but that Jacob possessed those necessary qualities. But her affection for Jacob supplanted what should have been her highest concern—right, truth, and honor. She ignored the feelings of Isaac, her husband, and Esau, her son. And in trying to help Jacob, she involved him in a serious crime.

Isaac's suspicion was first aroused by Jacob's quick arrival. "How did you find it so quickly?" he inquired. Caught off guard, Jacob had to lie and bring God into his answer. "The Lord your God gave me success," he responded. Isaac also recognized Jacob's voice, but the feel of the hairy hands and the smell of Esau on the clothes helped override his suspicions. Rebekah and Jacob carried out their deception successfully.

Rebekah's plan to obtain the blessing for her favorite son by using fraud worked. But it also backfired. She had told Jacob "let the curse fall on me," but she could not guarantee his safety after the deed. Infuriated, Esau vowed that as soon as Isaac was dead, he would kill Jacob. Rebekah's careless action alienated one son and imperiled the life of the other. Her quick mind had to devise another plan to save Jacob. But again she did not share her fears with Isaac. Perhaps he was in no mood to discuss anything with her. The inability to communicate showed again.

On one matter Isaac and Rebekah saw eye to eye. Esau had taken two Hittite wives, and both parents were grieved by the presence of these heathen women. Since there were two of them, they posed an increased religious threat. No doubt they brought their idols to their new home and openly worshipped them.

Using this one topic that they agreed on, Rebekah sought to get Jacob out of Esau's reach. She expressed the fear that Jacob might also marry a heathen woman and asked that he be allowed to go to her home in Haran to find a wife from among her people. Isaac readily agreed to the plan and himself charged Jacob, instructing him to go quickly.

Now, as Jacob prepared to leave, Isaac called him and gave him the blessing he wanted all along. He said, " 'May God Almighty bless you and make you fruitful and increase your numbers until you become a community of peoples. May he give you and your descendants the blessing given to Abraham, so that you may take possession of the land ... God gave to Abraham' " (Genesis 28:3, 4).

The earlier blessing that Isaac thought he was giving Esau only made Jacob lord over his brother. This unintentionally fulfilled the prophecy made by God before the birth of the twins (Genesis 25:23).

Silent Love: Isaac and Rebekah

But this new blessing included both the promise of numerous descendants and the promise of the land, mentioning becoming heir to the promise of Abraham. Perhaps Isaac knew all along what he was doing. Perhaps he had had no intention to pass the promises God made to Abraham on to Esau. In any case, the right blessing was kept waiting for Jacob. But if only he and Rebekah had talked it over, so much sadness could have been avoided.

---

1. For an insightful comparison see Robert Alter, *The Art of the Biblical Narrative*, 45.

CHAPTER 4

Ardent Love: Jacob and Rachel

In an age and culture that required parents to arrange the marriages of their children, Jacob and Rachel stand out as an example of love before marriage. Jacob loved Rachel so much that he was willing to do anything—cross any sea, climb any mountain, or accomplish any task—to obtain Rachel as his wife.

The Bible assumes that husbands will love wives, but very few are described as doing so. Abraham told Sarah how she could show her love to him, and she acceded to his request (Genesis 20:13). Michal, daughter of Saul, was in love with David (1 Samuel 18:20), though probably all the young women were his fans after he killed Goliath. Solomon loved all his foreign wives (1 Kings 11:2), but in a different sense. But Jacob's love exceeded all those. We have much evidence that Jacob loved Rachel with a really passionate love—the kind we respect.

Marrying within the family

The intermarriage of good people with evil (Genesis 6:1–3) was one sin that influenced God's decision to cleanse the earth by the Flood. The "sons of God," who married the daughters of men in Noah's day, were not angels, as some think (for Jesus plainly said in Mark 12:25 that angels do not marry), but God's holy people. Elsewhere, Moses referred to the Israelites as "children of the Lord your God" and strictly forbade them to follow the customs of the hea-

Ardent Love: Jacob and Rachel

then people around them (Deuteronomy 14:1). In his farewell song, Moses indicated that when they acted corruptly, the Israelites could not be called children of God (Deuteronomy 32:5). If the Flood was the result of intermarriage with unbelievers, it was no wonder that postdiluvian patriarchs took the matter of intermarriage very seriously.

Abraham's family went to great lengths to avoid marriage with unbelievers. To do this, they married within the family. This raised no eyebrows because it meant marrying within the faith. Jacob and Rachel's family tree had several marriages within the extended family. Nahor had married Milcah, his niece (Genesis 11:29). Commissioned by Abraham, Eliezer (Abraham's servant) fetched the great-granddaughter of Haran (Abraham's brother) for Isaac. Through his father, Jacob was an uncle of Laban. Through his mother, Laban was his uncle!

Relationship of Jacob and Rachel

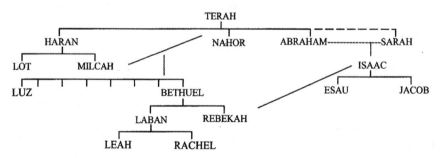

In contrast, Esau married outside the family and outside the faith to two Hittite women. This so grieved his parents (Genesis 26:34) that Rebekah eventually said to Isaac, " 'I'm disgusted with living because of these Hittite women. If Jacob takes a wife from among the women of this land, from Hittite women like these, my life will not be worth living' " (Genesis 27:46).

Rebekah used this pretext to move Jacob beyond the reach of Esau, who had sworn that as soon as Isaac died, he would kill Jacob for stealing his blessing (Genesis 27:41). But Rebekah's strategy worked. Isaac happily sent Jacob away with his blessing, instructing him not to marry a Canaanite but to go to his mother's family to

FOR BETTER OR FOR WORSE

seek a wife from among the daughters of Laban, his mother's brother (Genesis 28:1, 2). In retaliation, Esau married a third wife—this time the daughter of Ishmael (Genesis 28:9).

About sixty miles into the journey at a place called Luz, Jacob had his dream about the ladder reaching to heaven (Genesis 28:10–19). Renaming the place Bethel, he set out with renewed vigor for Haran, approximately four hundred miles farther northeast. Every time he came to a town, he asked what place it was and found he had farther to go. But finally he arrived at Haran. It was afternoon, and he saw a field with three flocks of sheep lying beside a well.

"Do you know Laban?" he inquired of the shepherds who had informed him he was in Haran. "Yes," they replied, and added, "here comes his daughter Rachel with his sheep."

Herds were Laban's life. He had named his first daughter "cow" and his second "ewe." Rachel, the ewe, possessed a lovely figure and a pretty face. Though Laban had several sons, Rachel was the family shepherdess (Genesis 29:9). Every afternoon she led the flock to the well. When all the flocks of the village had assembled, the shepherds would roll away the stone and water the animals. Not enough flocks had assembled this day for the stone to have been removed.

Jacob had been harboring guilt for cheating his brother and deceiving his father. He missed his mother and was tired from the long trek. Most of all he was lonely. When he saw his lovely cousin Rachel and realized that he was again near family, Jacob expressed his relief emotionally. Shoving the great stone aside, he watered her flock and kissed her, weeping as he informed her who he was.

Laban was excited to meet his nephew and made him feel at home with them. Jacob lived with them happily, and after a month, Laban offered to pay Jacob for his work. It is hard to imagine that Laban's intentions were simple generosity when he offered to pay Jacob. Even after having become Jacob's father-in-law, Laban cheated him at every turn. Most likely, Laban reasoned that Jacob was a good young fellow and would surely make a good husband for his daughter.

Ardent Love: Jacob and Rachel

Jacob, on the other hand, had fallen in love with Rachel, and only the lack of assets prevented him from asking for her hand in marriage. Laban's offer of wages presented the opportunity he needed.

The dowry and the bride price

Dowry in the Old Testament took several forms. The bride's father was involved—he gave a maidservant to his daughter at the time of marriage. Thus Sarah, Rebekah, Leah, and Rachel acquired handmaids (Genesis 16:1; 24:61; 29:24, 29). Also, if the father could afford it, he gave more. Caleb gave his daughter a field with springs (Judges 1:15), and Pharaoh gave his daughter a city (1 Kings 9:16). The dowry system gave the young couple something to start life with. It also provided a security for the bride, for in case of divorce the dowry had to be returned. Often daughters received no inheritance from their parents other than what they received at the time of their marriage. Jewelry and coins formed part of the bride's trousseau. The silver coins in Jesus' parable of the missing coin (Luke 15:8–10) were probably from her dowry.

The groom's side also was expected to give gifts to the bride and her family. This is not strictly dowry, but a bride price. Daughters, as can be seen from the examples of Rebekah and Rachel, were very useful to the parents. Once they were married, it was a loss to their father's house and a gain for the groom's family. The bride price was to compensate for this loss. Eliezer, on behalf of his master Abraham, gave gold and silver jewelry and expensive clothes to Rebekah and other costly gifts to her mother and Laban her brother.

The bride price varied according to the importance of the families. The determination of the groom also influenced its size. The lovesick prince of Shechem pleaded with Jacob, " 'Make the price for the bride and the gift I am to bring as great as you like, and I'll pay whatever you ask me. Only give me the girl as my wife' " (Genesis 34:12). Centuries later, Saul asked David to kill a hundred Philistines to earn the hand of his daughter Michal.

But the system had its dangers. A greedy father might demand an exorbitant sum and thus eliminate worthy grooms who had inadequate fortunes. The richest groom is not necessarily the best.

FOR BETTER OR FOR WORSE

Jacob had arrived penniless and had nothing to offer except labor, and he offered to work seven years for Rachel.

It seemed a good bargain to Jacob because he had nothing else to offer. Laban liked the deal too. Laban had observed Jacob and noted that he was a good worker. Moreover, as he admitted, he preferred to give Rachel to Jacob rather than to a heathen (Genesis 29:19).

Bonded by love

Jacob kept his end of the contract, but after the seven years he made a blunder. "Give me my wife," he requested. "My time is completed." He should have said, "Give me Rachel to marry," thus preventing Laban's deception. Laban kept Rachel back and gave Jacob Leah as a wife—concealed behind her veil and by the darkness of the night (Genesis 29:22–25).

When Laban offered the excuse that it was not the custom to give the younger daughter to be married before the elder, he was not lying. In the East it is important for the elder daughter to be married first. Many a time, though ready and anxious, the younger must wait till the older sister finds a suitor. If the marriage of the younger is allowed to take place first, the couple gives a gift to the older sister. But even if Laban had the feelings of Leah in mind, propriety demanded that Jacob should have been informed of the custom. Laban attempted to soothe Jacob's anger by offering Rachel for another seven years of service. It was a tough bargain.

As the local man, Laban would have had the support of the town's people. Jacob was the refugee. As the employer, Laban had Jacob at his mercy. Up to this time, Jacob had been paid nothing. Most of all, Jacob's love for Rachel held him captive to Laban. He thus had no option but to submit meekly to the treachery. Scripture records only a mild protest from the helpless young man. Though Laban required another seven years of service for Rachel, he made one concession by allowing the couple to marry as soon as the wedding festivities for Leah were over (Genesis 29:27, 28).

Rivalry with Leah

The warm love between Jacob and Rachel left Leah out in the cold. But God compensated her by opening her womb. In quick

Ardent Love: Jacob and Rachel

succession she bore four sons. But the names Leah gave them reflected her deep pain at not being loved as Rachel was. Reuben was named because " 'the LORD has seen my misery.' " Leah hoped that the birth of a son would cause her husband to love her (Genesis 29:32). She chose the name Simeon " 'because the LORD heard that I am not loved' " (Genesis 29:33). She named the third son Levi because, she thought, " 'Now at last my husband will become attached to me' " (Genesis 29:34). The fourth she named Judah in praise to the Lord. The fact that Leah felt the lack of affection suggests that Rachel enjoyed all that Leah was denied.

There is no indication that Leah mocked the barren Rachel the way Peninnah taunted Hannah, the beloved wife of Elkanah (1 Samuel 1:6), but the names Leah gave her sons no doubt added pain and guilt to the injury of Rachel's barrenness.

In response to the birth of Leah's sons, Rachel demanded of Jacob, "Give me children, or I'll die." These words proved ironic, as Rachel finally died in childbirth (Genesis 35:16–18). The competition between the two sisters led them to give their maidservants to Jacob as surrogates to bear sons for them. After Rachel's maidservant bore her second son, Rachel declared, " 'I have had a great struggle with my sister, and I have won' " (Genesis 30:8). Leah's maidservant then bore two sons whom Leah named "Good Fortune" and "Happy" (Genesis 30:9–12).

Perhaps Rachel sometimes wondered whether the way Leah was treated was somehow wrong. It was obvious that Jacob loved Rachel more. Of course, Rachel was the one whom Jacob chose and for whom he worked so hard. Leah had become his wife through trickery. Was Leah herself partly to blame by going along with her father's deceitful plan, or in that society, did a daughter have the opportunity to oppose her father's wishes?

Leah's struggle with Rachel for Jacob's affection and attention opened a new chapter with the introduction of mandrakes, a plant that was supposed to promote fertility. Leah's son Reuben discovered mandrakes in the wheat field and brought them to his mother (Genesis 30:14). Leah then bartered the roots with Rachel in exchange for a night with Jacob. Another two sons were born to her, but even their births failed to win Jacob's love. But God finally remembered

Rachel. When she bore a son, she named him Joseph, meaning "may he add" saying, " 'May the LORD add to me another son' " (Genesis 30:24). That request was granted, but tragically, Rachel died during the second childbirth.

Jacob cheated again

After Jacob completed his second seven-year contract to obtain Rachel, he and his father-in-law embarked in a new struggle. Laban had paid Jacob for fourteen years of service with his two daughters. Now Laban had to pay him for further service. Jacob agreed to work in exchange for all the sheep that were not fully white and the goats that were not fully dark. The speckled, spotted, and dark lambs would be his. Laban agreed readily but cunningly removed the speckled, spotted, and dark animals from the herd and sent them three days' journey away in the care of his sons (Genesis 30:31–36).

Like Rachel, Jacob resorted to superstition in an attempt to reach his goals. This superstition suggested that offspring would resemble whatever the mother looked at during pregnancy. Even today, in some parts of the world, an expectant mother views pictures of beautiful children, hoping the child she will bear might resemble it. So Jacob spread sticks, streaked by peeling the bark, at the watering troughs. This strategy seemed to work, and Jacob's herds increased quickly (Genesis 30:41–43). But God later informed Jacob in a dream the fertility of his herds was God's intervention to compensate him for Laban's unfair treatment. (Genesis 31:10–12).

Attempt to obtain compensation

When God instructed Jacob to return to his homeland, Rachel and Leah joined forces for once. They were united in their belief that their father had cheated their husband, and they readily agreed to return to Canaan with him.

But even the plans to return to Canaan included deception. Rachel stole her father's household gods while he was away shearing his sheep (Genesis 31:19). These gods do not appear to have had religious significance, nor did Rachel seem to reverence them. She even sat on them to hide them from her father (Genesis 31:34, 35). Neither did Jacob have any use for them. In the end he buried them under a tree near Shechem (Genesis 35:4).

Nuzi tablets reveal the value of those idols. They determined the right to inheritance, and in the case of a married daughter, ensured that her husband would receive the family property if the family gods were in their possession.

In stealing the household gods, Rachel was attempting to correct the wrong she felt her father had done in not compensating her husband adequately. All that they had, Jacob had earned. Laban had given them nothing. The theft was also an attempt to preempt her brothers' claim on their inheritance and to ensure that Jacob held the chief title to Laban's estate.[1] Her brothers already resented Jacob's prosperity (Genesis 31:1).

Jacob and Rachel in the book of Jeremiah

Despite the romance in the story of Jacob and Rachel, a thread of tragedy runs throughout. After his flight from Esau, Jacob never again saw his mother to whom he was so attached. A refugee, and at the mercy of his uncle/father-in-law, he was cheated and exploited. He gave seven years of faithful labor for the love of his life, only to be given the wrong woman in marriage. After Jacob worked long enough to marry her, Rachel remained barren for years while her unloved sister bore children regularly. All of them trembled with fear while returning home because of Esau's threat. Finally, Rachel died early and left a mourning husband and two young sons behind.

Jeremiah, the weeping prophet, used both Jacob and Rachel to illustrate difficulties that he envisioned for Israel. Concerning the future he said,

This is what the LORD says:

"A voice is heard in Ramah,
    mourning and great weeping,
Rachel weeping for her children
    and refusing to be comforted,
    because her children are no more" (Jeremiah 31:15).

Jeremiah was writing primarily about the exile and stated that it would last seventy years (Jeremiah 25:11; 29:10). The captivity would be a time of intense sorrow for Rachel had she been alive, or Rebekah, or Sarah too, for that matter. Any woman would cry if she saw her descendants persecuted. Rachel was probably the one mentioned because the Israelites were referred to as Jacob (Jeremiah 31:7, 11). But Jeremiah went on to add that Rachel need not weep because her children were going to return from the land of their enemy to their own country (Jeremiah 31:16–18).

Matthew, under inspiration, applied Jeremiah's prophecy to the time of Jesus' birth when Herod killed the young boys in Bethlehem (Matthew 2:16, 18). Ephraim and Manasseh, tribes of Rachel's son Joseph, were part of the northern kingdom far from Bethlehem. But Benjamin, Rachel's younger son, joined Judah in the south (2 Chronicles 11:1–3). However, many from the tribes of Ephraim and Manasseh settled in Jerusalem from the beginning (1 Chronicles 9:3). Again, any of the female descendants, such as Sarah or Rebekah, would have wept to see innocent babies murdered by Herod.

Jeremiah referred to a time of trouble for Jacob (Jeremiah 30:7). Jacob had many times of trouble, but perhaps the greatest was when he wrestled with the angel by the river Jabbok (Genesis 32:1–31).

Jeremiah was obviously referring to the suffering the Israelites would experience during the exile (Jeremiah 30:3). But we are also told of a great time of trouble that will be at the end of time (Daniel 12:1; Matthew 24:2–25). This time of trouble has many similarities with what Jacob went through on his journey back to Canaan. Jacob was aware that he had erred in stealing the birthright. He wondered if God had forgiven him and would protect him from his brother, who had vowed to kill him (Genesis 27:41; 32:6–12). He also wrestled with God and then clung to Him for a blessing. As evidence that the Being with whom he was wrestling was divine, God touched Jacob's hip, resulting in immediate pain and a permanent disability (Genesis 32:31). In that time of "Jacob's trouble" the remnant will also have a death decree over their heads, and knowing that probation has closed, will wonder, like Jacob, if they are on God's side (Matthew 24:2–25; Revelation 16).

Ardent Love: Jacob and Rachel

The story of Jacob and Rachel is a romantic tale. But like many romances, this had its share of trouble. The game Jacob and Rachel, in which a blindfolded Jacob tries to catch a Rachel who tries to elude him, illustrates their frustration. But though conditions were not always ideal, their love enabled them to endure all difficulties. Through the ages, people have admired the love that Jacob showed Rachel in so many ways.

Jacob had fallen in love with Rachel probably at first sight (Genesis 29:17). The record declares plainly that he loved her more than he loved Leah (Genesis 29:30). Throughout her life, Rachel received Jacob's special favor. When traveling fearfully toward Esau, he placed Rachel and Joseph in the most secure location at the very end of the procession (Genesis 33:2), and after her death, he continued to favor her sons. Jacob gave her son Joseph a coat of many colors (Genesis 37:3) and held back Benjamin when the others went to buy grain from Egypt (Genesis 42:3, 4), even though Benjamin was a grown man with ten sons of his own (Genesis 46:21). Rachel's early death did not diminish Jacob's love for her children, but rather heightened it.

---

1. Merril Unger, *Archaeology and the Old Testament* (Zondervan, 1977), 123.

CHAPTER 5

Supportive Love: Moses and Zipporah

Being the wife of a leader is not easy. She has to stay far enough out of the way to avoid attracting unwanted attention. From those shadows, she has to look out for the well-being of her husband, the leader. She also has to provide the emotional support that her husband, the leader, often cannot get anywhere else because he has no other equal. As the wife of a prominent person, she is bound to attract criticism, which she must ignore. Zipporah, Moses' wife, fulfilled these requirements admirably.

Moses is perhaps the best known of all Old Testament characters. Zipporah is one of the less known. Being a foreigner and one from a despised nation, she obviously remained as much in the background as was possible. Eldest of the seven girls in her family, she was named "Little Bird." There is certainly a transliteration connection between *Zipporah* and *sparrow*, though *Zipporah* is thought to refer to a swallow.

Almost nothing is recorded about the relationship between Moses and his wife. More is written about their relationship with in-laws. Traditionally, in-laws have to be treated with caution because they may be difficult to get along with. Even so, we may glean a few insights from those incidents.

Chivalry at the well rewarded

Like Jacob centuries earlier, Moses, after traveling a few hundred miles, arrived at a settlement in the wilderness. Both Jacob and Mo-

Supportive Love: Moses and Zipporah

ses had run for their lives, Jacob from his brother, Esau, and Moses from Pharaoh. Jacob had left home and come to his mother's relatives. Moses had fled from his home, too, but it was from a country where his people were in bondage. Moses, the only free one, had no other place on earth to call home.

The well, the source of water for the village, was usually a little way outside the settlement. This was a meeting point, the best place to view the village girls, whose duty it was to fetch water for the family and to water the family flock. At a well Jacob had met Rachel, Eliezer had spotted Rebekah, and now Moses met Zipporah.

From the beginning of his flight, Moses had headed for Midian. The land of Midian was named after a son of Abraham borne by Keturah (Genesis 25:1, 2). To preserve Isaac's rights, Abraham had sent Midian and his brothers east with gifts (Genesis 25:5, 6). Most of the Midianites lived east of the Gulf of Aqaba, south of the Moabites.

Sitting by the well in Midian, Moses observed that rough shepherds had not merely chased away the seven daughters of Jethro but had waited until the girls had drawn water for their flock, and then driven them away so they could water their own sheep with that water. This type of injustice Moses could not bear to see. The Bible says he "came to their rescue" (Exodus 2:17). This drive to avenge injustice is what had gotten him into trouble in Egypt. The New Testament reports, " 'He saw one of them being mistreated by an Egyptian, so he went to his defense and avenged him by killing the Egyptian' " (Acts 7:24).

After chasing away the ruffians at the well, Moses proceeded to water the flock. When the girls returned home, Reuel, their father asked them, " 'Why have you returned so early today?' " (Exodus 2:18). The fact that the girls habitually came home later testifies to the fact that they normally had to draw water several times before they could quench the thirst of their own flock.

The girls described Moses to their father as an "Egyptian," probably on the basis of his dress, which no doubt also lent authority to his actions, helping him to drive away the shepherds. What Moses did required courage. He was not only alone but also a foreigner. On the other hand, the shepherds knew that they were in the wrong and didn't challenge him.

Reuel, another name for Jethro (Exodus 2:18; 3:1), chided the girls for not inviting their hero home for a meal. This is probably what they wanted to do all along, but felt too shy. Moses was invited not only for a meal but to live with them. Zipporah, probably the eldest, was promised to Moses in marriage, and, in return, Moses took charge of his father-in-law's flock the way Jacob had done for Laban centuries earlier.

Doing her husband's job

While Moses and his family were on the way to Egypt, a frightening incident took place. They were returning to Egypt as a result of God's call to Moses to deliver His people. Moses had put his wife and two sons on a donkey and headed north. Moses walked beside them with his staff (Exodus 4:19, 20).

Suddenly, at an inn where they had stopped to rest, they encountered the Lord, who threatened to kill Moses. They instinctively knew what the trouble was. Eliezer had not yet been circumcised. Apparently, they had discussed this rite and had deliberately put it off. Quickly Zipporah grabbed a flint knife and performed the circumcision, thus averting God's anger (Exodus 4:25, 26).

Several peoples of the Ancient Near East practiced circumcision. Of the peoples of Canaan, the Israelites referred only to the Philistines as "uncircumcised." So it seems not to have been a new custom that God invented for His people. He just gave it new meaning. Whereas for many, it was a sign of marriage—performed when a man was wedded—God used it as a sign of "marriage" of a person and people to Him. God instructed Abraham to circumcise every male in his household on the eighth day (Genesis 17:9–14), signifying that they were His from infancy. Abraham was ninety-nine when this was carried out. All the males in his household, including Ishmael, were circumcised. As descendants of Abraham, the Midianites must have been acquainted with the rite.

The practice of circumcision was strong enough among Abraham's descendants that it was enforced for Hamor the Shechemite who desired to marry Dinah, the daughter of Jacob (Genesis 34:15–18), though the brothers who had insisted on it had sinister motives (Genesis 34:25, 26).

God treated the neglect of circumcision as a serious omission. The immediate context sheds light why this was so important to God. God had just instructed Moses to demand that Pharaoh

Supportive Love: Moses and Zipporah

release Israel, " ' "my firstborn son" ' " (Exodus 4:22). Because Pharaoh would not release God's "firstborn son," God threatened to kill Pharaoh's firstborn son. In the verses immediately following, we are informed that Moses had neglected to circumcise his son and that God threatened to kill Moses for it (Exodus 4:23–26).

Moses was not ignorant of God's requirement that all males in Israel be circumcised. Because he already had two sons, Gershom and Eliezer (Exodus 4:20; 18:3, 4), and the circumcision of only one turned away God's anger, the other had apparently been previously circumcised. The Israelites in Egypt must have continued the practice of circumcising their sons because they did not need reminders of either the need for, or the significance of, circumcision. So if the Israelites, who had remained faithful in this regard, had discovered that Moses their leader had not circumcised his own son, they would have lost respect for him. He would have had no moral ground for asking them to follow any of God's instructions.

As for Moses himself, he was on the threshold of a mission that was a matter of life and death for the Egyptians as well as for the Israelites. The Egyptians, backed up against a wall, might try to assassinate him. The Israelites, if their rescue was frustrated, might turn hostile to him. His personal safety lay totally in the hands of God. No detail of God's instruction for Moses' personal life must be overlooked. God could not tolerate any known open disobedience to any of His commands.

After performing the circumcision on her son, Zipporah touched the severed tissue to the feet of Moses and said, "Surely you are a bridegroom of blood." We are not told why Zipporah called Moses a "bridegroom of blood." Most likely circumcision was to Zipporah a "bloody" ritual. She had probably witnessed the circumcision of her older son and it repulsed her. Perhaps she herself had been the obstacle to the circumcision of the second son and therefore felt the responsibility on this occasion.

But even if she had tried to prevent the circumcision, Moses had no excuse. He was responsible for seeing that God's command was carried out. Whichever of them was at fault, Zipporah took it upon herself to perform the procedure, no matter how revolting it was to her. Even though she made her disgust evident to Moses, yet it was her quick thinking that saved her husband's life and career.

FOR BETTER OR FOR WORSE

Concern for overloaded husband

When Moses left Midian to return to Egypt, he had neglected to tell his father-in-law the real reason for his leaving. Perhaps he was afraid that Jethro might have tried to restrain him. For whatever reason, he had told him only that he wanted to see family members who were still alive. Aaron, whom he had just met in the wilderness, would have told him who else in the family was still alive, and it sparked a desire to meet others. Jethro said, " 'Go, and I wish you well' " (Exodus 4:18). The next time Moses and his father-in-law met, Moses was the leader of a nation on the move.

Before reaching Egypt, Moses sent Zipporah and his two sons home to Midian to spare them from having to endure the plagues and turmoil in Egypt. Later, during the Exodus, Jethro took Zipporah and his two grandsons and journeyed to meet Moses and the Israelites. As Zipporah listened to Moses' account and watched him in action, she grew concerned. Ellen White tells us that she observed his burdens sapping his strength, and "she made known her fears to Jethro, who suggested measures for his relief." He watched as Moses judged all the cases personally from morning till night (Exodus 18:13, 14). Moses, like many charismatic leaders, had neglected to distribute the work load.

Exodus 18:12 refers to the "elders of Israel" who came with Aaron to share a meal with Jethro. This presence of elders suggests that some sort of subleadership existed. Yet it was obvious to Jethro that they were underused. He sensed that their talents were not called upon.

So Jethro advised Moses to appoint leaders of thousands, hundreds, fifties, and tens who would judge minor matters and bring only difficult cases to him. Moses respected Jethro and listened to the good advice his father-in-law gave. After Moses implemented the advice, Jethro returned home.

Detested by in-laws

The Bible says that "Miriam and Aaron began to talk against Moses because of his Cushite wife, for he had married a Cushite" (Numbers 12:1).

Some have suggested that this Cushite wife is not Zipporah be-

Supportive Love: Moses and Zipporah

cause she was a Midianite, but a new wife that Moses might have taken after the possible death of Zipporah. There is no biblical evidence for a second marriage of Moses, which should certainly have been a big event had there been one. Cush is the area south of Egypt in what is today Ethiopia. Cush was the son of Ham (Genesis 10:6), but not the one on whom the curse of Ham fell. That lot fell on Canaan (Genesis 9:25–27). There is no other expression of racist feelings towards the Cushites in the Bible. On the other hand, the Midianites were condemned as enemies by God.

Because God had prevented him from cursing the Israelites directly, Balaam found the ideal solution. He knew that idolatry in the Israelite camp would bring God's curse upon the Israelites. He advised the Midianite and Moabite leaders to use their women to turn the hearts of the Israelite men away from God. Thus the Midianite women in particular were condemned by God (Numbers 31:15, 16).

The Lord ordered Moses to " 'Treat the Midianites as enemies and kill them' " (Numbers 25:16) because of what happened with Balaam. Again the Lord said to Moses, " 'Take vengeance on the Midianites' " (Numbers 31:1). One can only imagine how Zipporah the Midianite felt as her people brought a curse on Israel. Aaron and Miriam, or anyone else, if they thought of saying anything at that time, wisely kept quiet.

There is some way in which we might consider Zipporah the Midianite being referred to as a Cushite. Cushan is used as a parallel term for Midian and is perhaps even an older poetical term for Midian. Habakkuk, reviewing Israel's history in poetry, writes, "I saw the tents of Cushan in distress, / the dwellings of Midian in anguish" (Habakkuk 3:7).

Perhaps Miriam and Aaron in their aspersion on Zipporah (Numbers 12:1) are not referring to Ethiopia, but to her Midianite heritage. Whatever it was they said, it came as a result of feelings against her that they had harbored for some time.

The next verse (Numbers 12:2) presents the real issue in the attack on Moses. Miriam and Aaron were jealous. They said, " 'Has the LORD spoken only through Moses? . . . Hasn't he also spoken through us?' "

Apparently, Miriam and Aaron thought their authority had declined, and they connected this trend to the wife of Moses. She was the informant for her father Jethro, who had influenced Moses to appoint scores of leaders. Miriam and Aaron were bypassed in this new chain of command.

On the other hand, Aaron and Miriam may never have properly accepted the wife of their brother and, after seeing her family in the wilderness, they may have despised her even more. Miriam and Aaron's attack on Moses was so serious that God intervened to chastise them.

Help from the brother-in-law

As they left the area near Midian, Moses said to Hobab, his brother-in-law, " 'We are setting out for the place about which the LORD said, "I will give it to you." Come with us and we will treat you well, for the LORD has promised good things to Israel' " (Numbers 10:29).

Some older versions of the Bible, in Judges 4:11, refer to Hobab as the father-in-law of Moses, but newer versions have corrected it to brother-in-law. In Numbers 10:29, "Now Moses said to Hobab son of Reuel the Midianite, Moses' father-in-law," it is unclear whether the father-in-law of Moses is Hobab or Reuel. But Exodus 2:18 makes it clear that Reuel is the father-in-law of Moses, and Hobab is his son and the brother-in-law of Moses.

If Hobab acceded to the request of Moses, he and his family would share in the blessings promised by God for Israel. Their presence would also provide family for Zipporah, Moses' wife. But Hobab's initial response was negative. He wanted to go back to his own land and his own people (Numbers 10:30).

From the stories Moses and Zipporah had told Hobab, it was clear that God had His hand over the Israelites. The future held great promise for them. But, it was a tough life being on the move. Though Moses, their leader, was his brother-in-law, it was not an easy decision to leave the comforts of home and of his people and cast his lot with the nomadic multitude.

But Moses pleaded again with Hobab and revealed a secondary motive for the invitation. He wanted Hobab to show them the best

Supportive Love: Moses and Zipporah

camping spots and to be their advisor in their journey through the desert (Numbers 10:31).

God guided the Israelites in deciding when to move and when to stop and set up camp through the movement of the cloud (Numbers 9:17). Whether it was two days or a month, they remained in one place as long as the cloud stayed put. But Hobab could guide them to the best camping spot in the area; he might know the location of the closest springs or wells and what dangers might be near. His advice would not compete with God's guidance through the cloud, but complement it.

The Bible does not record the final decision of Hobab. He must have acceded to Moses' request. Speaking of Heber, the Bible tells us that he "had left the other Kenites, the descendants of Hobab, Moses' brother-in-law" (Judges 4:11). At the time of Jeremiah, a group of Recabites had left their tents and migrated to Jerusalem. These Recabites were highly commended by God for their faithfulness during the final days of Judah (Jeremiah 35:1–19). The chronicler informs us that the Recabites are Kenites (1 Chronicles 2:55). Hobab must have joined the Israelites. Some of his descendants stayed with Israel until the Babylonian captivity.

Hints from the book of Judges suggest that Hobab may have gone back to Midian after helping Moses guide Israel through the desert. Some of his descendants settled in Kedesh (Judges 4:11). Sisera, the commander of Jabin's army fleeing from Deborah and Barak, took refuge there in the tent of Jael, wife of Heber the Kenite. Though there was peace between Jabin and Heber (Judges 4:17), Jael had strong loyalties to Israel and killed Sisera while he slept.

The burden of Moses' leadership could have added an extra strain to the marriage, but Zipporah willingly shared her husband with the nation and showed the right balance of maintaining a low profile while at the same time providing the necessary support to the great leader. Zipporah placed no selfish demands on Moses that distracted him from devoting his full energy to his God-given task.

---

*Ellen White, *Patriarchs and Prophets*, 384.

CHAPTER 6

Stupid Love: Samson and Delilah

Many people confuse emotional attraction with love. Often the one experiencing that kind of "love" hardly knows the other person and is actually in love with an idealized imaginary image of that individual. Samson is a prime example because "he saw" and "he loved" without really getting to know the young woman. That kind of love is better known as infatuation.

The Latin word *fatuus* gave us our English word *infatuation*, which means "unintelligent." Its synonyms include *foolish*, *inane*, *silly*, and *stupid*. In the name of love, and for the sake of love, Samson did numerous stupid things.

Though Samson did not marry Delilah, it is her name, rather than that of his unidentified wife, that has become associated with his. Samson was married some time earlier, and there are many striking similarities in the experience Samson had with the woman he had married (Judges 14) and with Delilah, the woman with whom he later fell in love (Judges 16).

1. Both women were Philistines (Judges 14:2; 16:4).
2. Both were recruited by Philistines to snare Samson (Judges 14:15; 16:5).
3. Both coaxed him, using manipulation similar to "If you love me . . ." (Judges 14:16; 16:15).
4. Both attempts were initially resisted by Samson (Judges 14:16; 16:10, 13, 15).

Stupid Love: Samson and Delilah

5. Both were ultimately successful in learning his secret (Judges 14:17; 16:17).

On the way to his wedding with the earlier Philistine woman, Samson had spotted a colony of bees in a lion carcass, which inspired a riddle he posed to his Philistine guests. He bet that they would not solve it within the seven days of the wedding feast. The wager involved thirty sets of clothing. Threatened by the guests, his bride wheedled and nagged Samson till he stupidly told her the answer. Before the deadline, the Philistines recited the answer to Samson, who became furious when he realized that his bride had betrayed his love.

Falling in love

The Bible recounts that some time later, Samson "fell in love" with Delilah, the second Philistine woman (Judges 16:4).

The NIV renders the Hebrew "he loved" as "he fell in love." *Falling* has negative connotations. Falling is unplanned and unintentional. No one wants to fall; it hurts. What we want is to get up and get going. We can prevent falls by being alert to the dangers that surround us.

Figurative "falls" are equally tragic. They may describe loss of position. We speak of "the Fall" when we refer to the first sin of Adam and Eve. We also refer to Satan's fall from heaven, which means more than just being cast down to the earth. David described the death of Saul and Jonathan with the statement " 'How have the mighty fallen' " (2 Samuel 1:25, 27). The term *fall* is very appropriate for Samson, the strongest man who ever lived.

Samson is one of the few characters in the Bible described as "falling in love." (Amnon, who fell in love with his sister, Tamar, was another.) This is not merely an event in Samson's life, but a way of life with him.

Samson's emotions were guided solely by physical appearances. The first time he said to his parents, " 'I have *seen* a Philistine woman in Timnah; now get her for me as my wife' " (Judges 14:1, 2, italics added). Later he *saw* a Philistine prostitute in Gaza and went to spend the night with her (Judges 16:1). Marrying someone about whom one knows little, except how she looks, is like buying a product based only on the attractiveness of the label. One can usually return a purchase if dissatisfied with a product, but marriage is meant to be for keeps.

Samson was more stupid than his Philistine father-in-law expected. After his wife betrayed him and ruined the wedding week, Samson stormed out in anger. The bride's father understandably assumed that Samson would not return, and he gave the young woman to the best man (Judges 14:20). He didn't reckon with Samson's stupidity. Even though she had proved to be a traitor, Samson later arrived to reunite with her, bringing a young goat as a peace offering (Judges 15:1).

But Samson did learn one thing from his first marriage—not to get married till he knew someone quite well. Samson had fallen in love with Delilah readily enough without getting to know her, but at least he did not marry her. He visited her at least four times, probably more. With each visit it became more obvious that she was the same type as the woman he had married earlier. He should have remembered his experience with his wife as soon as Delilah showed similar traits of character, wheedling and begging for his secret and repeatedly betraying him. He couldn't help falling in love, but he had avoided falling into marriage. Nevertheless, by flirting with danger, he had a much bigger fall.

The folly of intermarriage

When Samson urged his parents to arrange his marriage with the earlier Philistine woman, they replied, " 'Isn't there an acceptable woman among your relatives or among all our people? Must you go to the uncircumcised Philistines to get a wife?' " (Judges 14:3). Of all the nations in Canaan, only the Philistines were referred to as the "uncircumcised," and therefore as totally heathen (Judges 14:3; 15:18; 1 Samuel 14:6; 17:26, 36; 31:4; 2 Samuel 1:20; 1 Chronicles 10:4). The alliances of Samson with Philistine women no doubt caused his parents deep concern (Judges 14:3, 4).

The Old Testament contains numerous warnings about the

Stupid Love: Samson and Delilah

dangers of intermarriage between Israelites and the people of other nations. When Moses led the Israelites to the threshold of the Promised Land, God warned them about the Canaanites and all the other "ites." He instructed the Israelites not to make treaties with them, to smash the objects of their worship, and not to allow their sons to take Canaanite women, who prostituted themselves to their gods because " 'they will lead your sons to do the same' " (Exodus 34:10–16). The list of seven banned nations (Deuteronomy 7:1) is probably not meant to be comprehensive, but illustrative, because the list of nations into which Solomon wrongly married included several not listed by Moses (1 Kings 11:1–6).

The Israelites disregarded God's instructions. They not only took in marriage Canaanite daughters but also gave their own daughters in marriage to Canaanite sons with the result that their children served other gods (Judges 3:5, 6).

Solomon later outdid all in the matter of intermarriage. Ahab's marriage had the worst results for himself and for the nation. Especially during the Babylonian exile, scores, including priests, married women from the banned nations. Ezra's men compiled a list of all the guilty (Ezra 9; 10), and Nehemiah banned from his presence a certain priest guilty of intermarriage (Nehemiah 13:28–30).

Though Samson was quick to associate with people outside his faith, yet, he never openly wavered in his loyalty to his religion. Samson frequented the Philistine towns west of his home, and he easily formed alliances with the women who caught his fancy there but without thought of worshiping their gods.

But while Samson did not worship foreign gods, his disobedience to Yahweh's laws still resulted in suffering. He allowed his long hair, the Nazirite symbol of his dedication to Yahweh, to be cut. The removal of this symbol forfeited God's special blessing on Samson manifested in his astonishing physical strength. Samson revealed this secret to Delilah, surely knowing that she would follow through with betrayal as in the other times. Armed with the knowledge of his secret, she became the instrument for the separation of God from Samson.

FOR BETTER OR FOR WORSE

If you love me

Both of Samson's Philistine women pried out his secrets by questioning his love. The veiled threat was the equivalent of "if you don't tell me, you can't claim to love me and therefore you can't claim my love." Samson's wife had said, " 'You don't really love me. . . . you haven't told me . . .'" (Judges 14:16). Delilah had said to him, " 'How can you say, "I love you," when you won't confide in me?' " (Judges 16:15).

How often have we heard these words, "If you love me, you will . . ."? This saying represents a refusal to accept love on the terms it is being given, and instead wants it on the terms of the receiver. The lover is being indirectly informed that their relationship is dependent on some significant sacrifice.

Delilah expected Samson to part with the secret of his strength. " 'Tell me the secret of your great strength and how you can be tied up and subdued,' " Delilah purred (Judges 16:6). The second part of her request "and how you can . . . be subdued" suggested that she did not want to know his secret merely in admiration of his great strength but that she intended for him to be overcome. Again and again Samson gave her wrong information, and each time she tested his word with an attempt to have him captured. But even after her treachery was exposed again and again, she still had the audacity to say, "If you really loved me, you would tell me your secret." The flow of the story causes the reader to cry out in response to Delilah, "You are the one lacking love, not he!"

Alarm bells should have gone off in Samson's head. He had heard something with the same ring before. His Philistine wife had wheedled the solution to his riddle out of him with the words "You hate me. You don't really love me." She cried the entire seven days of the wedding, until he broke down.

Just as Samson's wife wanted the answer to pass on to the Philistines, Delilah wanted the secret of his strength to relay to the Philistines who desired to kill him (Judges 14:15; 16:5). For the first miscalculation, Samson had to pay thirty garments to those who solved his riddle with his wife's help. Because Samson took the garments from the Philistines he butchered, he lost nothing except prestige.

Stupid Love: Samson and Delilah

The stakes were higher the second time—he was playing for his life.

As frequently happens, the infatuation is strong enough that the lover cannot bear for the relationship to end and so is willing to make a tragic sacrifice. An observer viewing the situations objectively can see the folly in surrender. But one blindly in love cannot measure values objectively. Samson made the same mistake despite having been lured once before, or perhaps because of that. He had come away from the first experience without any loss. In fact, he made the Philistines "pay" for his mistake. The second time, he paid with his life for his mistake. There can be a price for blind infatuation.

The secret of Samson's strength

Delilah wanted to know the secret of Samson's great strength, which had its actual origin in God. As Samson grew, the Spirit of the Lord began to stir in him (Judges 13:24). On the way to meet his prospective bride, the Spirit of the Lord came upon him in power, and he was able to kill a lion (Judges 14:6). After his wife betrayed him and he had to pay thirty sets of garments, the Spirit of the Lord came upon him in power, and he killed thirty Philistines whose robes he took to pay those who answered his riddle (Judges 14:19). Once when the Spirit of the Lord came upon him in power, he struck down a thousand Philistines who came to arrest him (Judges 15:14). But finally, when the Spirit of the Lord left him, Samson's physical power disappeared (Judges 16:20, 21).

Even before his birth, God had instructed that Samson should be a Nazirite, which signified that he was dedicated to God (Judges 13:5). Normally, a man or woman made his or her own decision to take the Nazirite vows. At times the parents dedicated their child to God as Nazirite. In Samson's case, God made the selection before he was born. But even though Samson did not make the initial choice to be a Nazirite, he could choose to abandon the relationship.

Numbers 6:1–12 provides details for one undertaking Nazirite vows of dedication to God. It involved the following restrictions:
1. Abstaining from strong drink—wine, vinegar, or anything fermented.

2. Not eating anything from the vine—grapes, raisins, skins, or seeds.
3. Not shaving the head, but letting the hair grow long.
4. Not going near a dead body.

The vows are normally taken for a specified period of time (Numbers 6:5, 8, 13). Even if a family member died, the Nazirite was not to defile his consecration by going near the body. And if someone died suddenly in his or her presence, the Nazirite was automatically defiled. The Nazirite had to cut off his hair, offer doves as a sin offering and burnt offering, sacrifice a lamb, and begin the period of consecration all over again. The long hair was understood to be the visible symbol of consecration to God. Samson's long hair was tied in seven braids (Judges 16:19).

Bluffing, but edging closer

When Delilah pressed him to tell her the secret of his great strength, Samson lied, giving her different answers each time, but edging closer and closer to the truth with each round. The first time he told her that if he were tied with seven fresh leather thongs that had not been tanned, he could be overcome. There was a slight connection with the secret. His long hair was tied in seven braids, seven, perhaps, in connection with his covenant with God. The second time Samson told her that if she used seven new ropes he'd lose his strength. He seemed now to be hinting that the secret had to do with something braided. The third time he said that the secret had something to do with his hair, though he made up the part about weaving it into the weaver's loom. Each time, he surrendered a little more of his precious secret.

The stupidity of Samson is glaring when time after time Delilah beckoned the Philistines to come and capture him. When they failed repeatedly, the woman didn't give up in shame but brazenly shed crocodile tears and complained, "You've made me a fool. You don't really love me." And she plagued him again. And he came closer and closer to the truth, perhaps smug because of his previous escape. Like the moth flirting with the candle and getting closer and closer to the flame until it is singed, Samson flirted with danger, getting

Stupid Love: Samson and Delilah

closer and closer to being snared. Unable to resist Delilah, he divulged his secret in full. He told everything about his consecration to God and his long hair as the symbol. If it were cut, he told her, he'd lose his strength (Judges 16:17).

Stupid guy. At least Samson should have left after giving up his secret. Even if he stayed, he should have remained awake. The Philistines were no match for him while he was awake. If he had to sleep, he should have locked the door. If he'd run away or been on the alert after that so nobody could get to his hair, we'd give him a bit of credit. But Samson let down his guard and went to sleep. Amazingly foolish.

Next it was Delilah's turn to make a fool of Samson. No words that she might have spoken are recorded. But she put him, the unsuspecting champion, the strongest man who ever lived, to sleep on her lap, a place to lay your head and sleep only when you trust completely. So sure was she that she now knew Samson's secret, that she collected the silver she was promised even before she called in the barber to shave his head (Judges 16:18, 19).

Betraying love for money

The rulers of the Philistines had promised Delilah that if she could lure Samson into revealing the secret of his great strength and how they could overpower him, each would pay her " 'eleven hundred shekels of silver' " (Judges 16:5).

Because there were five Philistine lords (Judges 3:3), the sum offered to Delilah would total fifty-five hundred shekels of silver. Thirty shekels bought a slave (Exodus 21:32), so Delilah could have purchased 170 slaves with that money. In terms of weight, the rulers offered her about one hundred pounds of silver.

Delilah played for money. Samson played for love. But the game was rendered unequal by the different intensities of their love. Obviously, Samson could not bear to give up Delilah. On the other hand, Delilah could bear to give up Samson and did, for money. Both were playing a game of deceit, Samson concealing the secret of his strength, and Delilah hiding the reason she wanted to know the secret of his strength. Because she played for money, Delilah's name today is associated with the betrayal of love for material gain. One wonders how much was necessary for her to betray her lover. The Philistines didn't take any chances. They offered her a sum so large, it ensured her compliance.

Samson's great physical strength was matched only by his weakness for women that made him do stupid things. From experience after experience, the Philistines knew that he could never be overcome with power. They also knew his great weakness and tapped into it. For indulging in his weakness, he paid a high price. First he lost his freedom. Then he lost his sight. Ironically his eyes, which got him into infatuation with beauty and lust, were put out. Finally, he paid with his life.

Incredibly stupid guy! At any time he could have walked away from Delilah to freedom. But he was trapped by his infatuation. Samson went to sleep on her lap, knowing that he was placing his life in the hands of one who had repeatedly demonstrated her intention to betray him.

CHAPTER 7

Selfless Love: Boaz and Ruth

We would expect the generation of Israelites in the land of Canaan after the Exodus to gratefully settle down in the Promised Land to a life of service to God and faithful witness to the surrounding nations. But no, they turned out to be just as evil as their neighbors. The book of Judges concludes with this statement: "In those days Israel had no king; everyone did as he saw fit" (Judges 21:25).

Abandoning God's guidelines for living, they indulged in violence and disobedience. But against this background of selfishness, the refreshing love story of Boaz and Ruth shows how selfless love can inspire an entire town.

Ruth, a despised Moabite, demonstrated a faithful love to her bereaved mother-in-law and her God and won the hearts of the Bethlehemites. Boaz, who might have given up the idea of marriage, also showed consistent generosity to Ruth and Naomi.

The story begins with a natural disaster. A famine had driven Elimelech and his family—his wife, Naomi, and their sons, Mahlon and Kilion—to the land of Moab on the other side of the Dead Sea. A temporary period of peace seems to have prevailed during this time, making emigration possible. While they escaped the famine, they couldn't elude tragedy. First Elimelech died. Then the two sons, who by now had married local women, also died (Ruth 1:1–5).

FOR BETTER OR FOR WORSE

The story could have ended with the three deaths, but instead, it begins here—the story of the beauty of Ruth's selfless love. She could have despaired at the tough life she'd been meted out and her bleak future as a widow, with little to look forward to. She could have listened to Moabites who told her that she had married into a family that was marked, that the God of Israel was either impotent or angry with them.

Naomi's decision to return to Bethlehem provided the right opportunity for Ruth to break with her and return to her own family, the way Orpah did. That does not mean that Orpah was not a good person. She too showed fine character. Apparently, she had been a good wife to Kilion. She enjoyed a good relationship with Naomi and even started out on the road to Judah with Naomi and Ruth. Only at Naomi's urging did she return to her own home. Orpah was a good person, but Ruth's thoughtful love shines so much stronger that Orpah is overshadowed.

Loving daughter-in-law

In response to Naomi's suggestion to return to her people, Ruth said, " 'Where you go I will go, and where you stay I will stay. Your people will be my people and your God my God. Where you die I will die, and there will I be buried' " (Ruth 1:16, 17).

She was not being fatalistic, but she was absolutely firm. She intended to stick by her mother-in-law come what may.

The entire village could tell that Ruth's motives were genuine. Boaz told her, " 'I've been told all about what you have done for your mother-in-law since the death of your husband—how you left your father and mother and your homeland and came to live with a people you did not know before' " (Ruth 2:11).

Ruth was thinking, not of herself, but of Naomi; not of who would look after her, but of how she could care for her mother-in-law; not of her Moabite friends and family, but of Naomi's. Her mother-in-law had no wealth or security to offer her, but Ruth had observed the family and had fallen in love with them and with their God.

The lovely relationship between Ruth and her mother-in-law is refreshing. So many unkind jokes have been told about mothers-in-

Selfless Love: Boaz and Ruth

law. So many family arguments have revolved around mothers-in-law that caution must be exercised when mentioning them. Even when mothers-in-law mean well and act out of love, they are often easily misunderstood as interfering. Spouses are often caught between two people they love and who love them. Ruth and Orpah were close to their mother-in-law after their husbands' deaths, though we get the impression that the relationship was good all along.

Dutiful daughter-in-law

The two women arrived in Bethlehem as the barley harvest was beginning (Ruth 1:22). Grain was normally cut by men with hand sickles (Jeremiah 50:16; Joel 3:13), collected on the arm (Psalm 129:7), and then tied into sheaves by young women (Ruth 2:8). The Law of Moses directed owners of fields not to harvest the corners of the field, but to leave some at the edges for the poor. Also, any stalks left standing after the reapers had gone through the field once could be gleaned by the needy (Leviticus 19:9; 23:22; Deuteronomy 24:19).

Ruth immediately understood the opportunity for collecting food for Naomi and herself. Ruth did not even think of letting the older woman go out to glean. It would have been natural to expect Naomi to provide for the foreigner, but Ruth spared her mother-in-law the task and took the initiative. She requested Naomi to let her glean in the field of anyone who allowed it.

Gleaning sounds like easy work—simply picking up grain that has been intentionally left. It was not as easy at it sounds. Ruth would repeatedly have had to bend over and straighten up, picking up the stalks. The harvest-time sun would have beat down on her relentlessly. Her arm would have tired with the weight of stalks. Then she would have had to beat the grain to thresh it (Ruth 2:17). Then she would have had to collect the grain into her garment, which would have become heavier and heavier.

In addition, the fields were planted outside the city at a considerable distance. Therefore, there were dangers for a young foreign woman spending time in them. Yet Ruth took the risk in going out to glean food to provide for Naomi (Ruth 2:2). Her generous love for her mother-in-law is further seen in that she also took home food from what had been given to her for her own lunch (Ruth 2:18).

Generosity of Boaz

When Boaz found out the identity of the young woman gleaning in his field, he did several thoughtful things. (1) He gave her full encouragement to glean in his fields, instructing her not to go to any other fields. As a member of the clan of Elimelech (Ruth 2:1), Boaz's fields were probably conveniently close to Naomi's. (2) He provided for her peace of mind by informing her that the men had been instructed not to bother her. This is exactly what Naomi had been worrying about (Ruth 2:22). (3) He further provided for her needs by making his supply of drinking water available for her. Water supplied near the fields meant that Ruth didn't have to choose between becoming dehydrated in the hot sun or losing time by going for a drink (Ruth 2:8, 9).

Boaz further tried to avoid making Ruth feel like she was a beggar. At mealtimes he invited her to join his harvesters for bread and a relish made with vinegar and even gave her enough roasted grain so that there were leftovers. He instructed his men not to embarrass her if she gleaned among the tied sheaves and even told them to deliberately remove stalks of grain from the sheaves and drop some on the ground for her to find. The amount that Ruth took home was more than could be gained through mere hard work. It testified to generosity. Finally, Boaz invited her to spend the rest of the harvest days in his fields (Ruth 2:14–21).

Providence of God

The record says: "As it turned out, she found herself working in a field belonging to Boaz, who was from the clan of Elimelech" (Ruth 2:3).

We understand that in the beginning of the story, the odds of Ruth ending up marrying Boaz were indeed minuscule. Many circumstantial events were necessary to lead to their eventual meeting and marriage.

1. There had to be a famine in Judah; otherwise the family of Elimelech would not have left Bethlehem.

Selfless Love: Boaz and Ruth

2. They had to choose Moab for refuge rather than some other country, such as Egypt or Edom, in order to come in contact with Ruth.
3. There had to be eligible men in Naomi's family to marry Ruth.
4. The husband had to die in order for Ruth to be eligible for a second marriage.
5. The famine in Judah had to end so Naomi could consider going back.
6. Ruth had to decide to accompany Naomi.
7. Ruth had to happen to glean in the field of Boaz.

The Hebrew has a double use of the term for *chance*. Literally it means "her chance chanced." Today we might say, "As luck had it, she happened to . . ." It seems almost profane to suggest in such a story that it was mere chance that brought Ruth to the field of Boaz. We would prefer the term *providence*.

Thoughtfulness of Naomi

Naomi earnestly sought the best for her daughter-in-law, and Ruth realized and appreciated it. They had been in Bethlehem only a short time—the harvest was just ending. The young widow Ruth had daily returned from the fields with a load of grain and stories of Boaz's generosity. The older widow was on the lookout for her daughter-in-law and sensed an opportunity to provide for her future.

So far in the story, it has been Ruth who provided for Naomi. Now, halfway into the story, Naomi will provide for Ruth. "Fate" may have brought Ruth to the field of Boaz. But for the next step, Naomi will leave nothing to chance.

At this point Naomi suggested an interesting way of "proposing" to Boaz. Ruth was to wash and perfume herself and dress in her best clothes. At night she was to sneak up to where Boaz lay and curl up at his feet. When Boaz awoke, she was to request him to cover her with the corner (literally, *wings*) of his garment.

Apparently, the act of covering with the corner of the garment was a marriage ritual. When Moses commanded that a man should not marry his father's wife, what he literally said in Hebrew was "a man was not to uncover the corner of his father's garment" (see Deuteronomy 22:30). The prophet Ezekiel, describing God's marriage with His people, used similar terminology as in this story of Ruth. God said, " 'I spread the corner of my garment over you.' " Ezekiel also mentions a washing and cleansing of God's people, and a putting on of their best clothes (Ezekiel 16:8–10).

Kindness of Boaz

Though it was made in the darkness of the night, the proposal had the potential to be embarrassing for Ruth. Someone could have seen her and spread rumors, ruining her reputation. Boaz might have refused her request. He was a confirmed bachelor and perhaps didn't want to marry.

Boaz apparently was considerably older than Ruth. He had inquired of his men about her, referring to her as the "young woman" (Ruth 2:5). When he had spoken to Ruth, he addressed her as "my daughter" (Ruth 2:8; 3:11). This is what Naomi naturally had called her too (Ruth 1:12, 13; 2:22; 3:1). Boaz may have been closer in age to Naomi than to Ruth. He was impressed that she had not shown any interest in the young men and considered her interest in him a kindness on her part. Boaz made Ruth feel as if she was doing him a favor by proposing to him.

The response of Boaz parallels God's dealing with Israel revealed in the book of Ezekiel. Boaz promised Ruth he would do all she asked (Ruth 3:11–13). This corresponds to the oath in Ezekiel 16:8. In the morning Boaz sent Ruth back to Naomi laden with food (Ruth 3:15). Similarly, God provided His bride Israel with fine flour, honey, and olive oil (Ezekiel 16:13).

Boaz's action was not without some thought of sacrifice. Marrying someone else's childless widow carried risks. The nearer kinsman referred to this when he said, " 'Then I cannot redeem it because I might endanger my own estate' " (Ruth 4:6). But Boaz was still willing to care for and provide for Ruth.

Commitment to God

One may wonder how such selfless love could exist in such a horrible period as the time of the judges. The answer is simple. It had

Selfless Love: Boaz and Ruth

its origin in Ruth, Naomi, and Boaz's commitment to God. Ruth had opportunity to learn about the God of Israel from her husband before he died and from her in-laws. She liked what she saw and she told Naomi, " 'Your people will be my people and your God my God' " (Ruth 1:16).

This was not as simple as it might sound. Edomites and Egyptians were not considered totally corrupt. The Israelites were instructed to be more tolerant to them. The great-grandchildren (the third generation) of Edomites and Egyptians might be allowed into the assembly of the Lord (Deuteronomy 23:7, 8). But no descendant of any Ammonite or Moabite could enter the Lord's assembly even down to the tenth generation (Deuteronomy 23:3). This phrase might be taken to mean "never ever" (Deuteronomy 23:6).

The Moabites and Midianites had hired Balaam to curse Israel (Numbers 22:4–6). When Balaam's plan A failed, he suggested plan B, which involved using Moabite and Midianite women to seduce the Israelites into immorality. The plot worked and brought the curse of God on His own people (Numbers 25:1–3). That is why God forbade the Israelites from intermarrying with the Moabites.

The Law of Moses declared that if anyone entered into any type of forbidden marriage, their descendants down to the tenth generation would be barred from entering God's assembly (Deuteronomy 23:3). Deuteronomy mentions seven nations on the banned list (Deuteronomy 7:1–3). This list is not comprehensive but only illustrative. Moab is not on the list. Yet Solomon is condemned for marrying wives from a list of banned nations that included Moab (1 Kings 11:1, 2). David and Solomon were descendants of Ruth and less than ten generations down the line. Theoretically, they should have been barred from entering God's presence. But Ruth had adopted Naomi's God as her very own and, in return, God accepted her and allowed her to be an ancestor of His own Son (Matthew 1:5–16).

Boaz blessed Ruth, saying, " 'May you be richly rewarded by the Lord, the God of Israel, under whose wings you have come to take refuge' " (Ruth 2:12). He likened Ruth's approach to Yahweh as a surrender and request for refuge.

We see many indications that Boaz, too, was a God-fearing individual. His greeting to his harvesters was, " 'The Lord be with you!' " and their response to him was, " 'The LORD bless you!' " (Ruth 2:4).

The angel who appeared to Gideon and to Mary greeted them similarly, saying, " 'The LORD is with you' " (Judges 6:12; Luke 1:28). This appears to have been Boaz's customary salutation. The context implies a bountiful harvest, which benefits both the owner and the laborers of the fields. An opposite situation is imagined in Psalm 129:7, 8. The harvest was poor, the reapers' hands were empty, and passers-by could not say, " 'The blessing of the LORD be upon you.' "

This exchange of greetings tells us several things about Boaz's religion. (1) Boaz was a godly man. (2) He shared his religion with his workers. (3) His workers responded to his religious nature. There seems to have been a good working relationship between employer and workers based on their common dependence on God.

Risks of being a kinsman-redeemer

Redemption is perhaps the most important theme in the book of Ruth. In various forms, the Hebrew word occurs twenty-three times in these four chapters. A kinsman-redeemer performed several functions in Hebrew society. He was to redeem property that had been sold (Leviticus 25:25), to redeem relatives sold into servitude (Leviticus 25:47, 48), to avenge murder (Numbers 35:18, 19), and to assist in producing an heir for a married brother who died without having a son.

The last act has been called levirate marriage. *Levir* means "brother of a husband" (brother-in-law). The custom of a male relative marrying the deceased's widow to raise up an inheritance existed in other countries of the Ancient Near East as well. Deuteronomy 25:5 specifies that in Israel this practice applied just to brothers living together, but it is apparent that an extension of this principle was practiced, and in order of nearness of kin.

Naomi had not sold the family property, but if and when it did go up for sale, the closest relatives would have the first option to buy it so as to keep it in the family. The kinsman who would redeem this also had the obligation to marry Ruth to provide an heir for Mahlon, her deceased husband.

Selfless Love: Boaz and Ruth

Naomi and Ruth had a closer unnamed kinsman, but he refused to redeem Naomi's property (Ruth 4:6) and take the risks involved. If the kinsman-redeemer had only one child, and that by Ruth, his own property would pass on in the name of Mahlon. Hence the law allowed the nearest kin the opportunity to refuse to do what was expected of him. However, the one who refused to redeem his relative's property and name was to undergo a humiliating ceremony (Deuteronomy 25:7–10). There is no record of this being done to the nearer kinsman.

But interestingly, even though no other offspring is mentioned for Ruth and Boaz, Obed, the son born to them, is listed in all genealogies as the son of Boaz and not as the son of the deceased former husband (Ruth 4:21; 1 Chronicles 2:12; Matthew 1:5; Luke 3:32).

The marriage of Boaz and Ruth did nothing to diminish the beautiful relationship between Naomi and Ruth. Naomi remained a part of the family. She was Ruth's former mother-in-law, and Ruth possibly had a new one. But Boaz is her relative and performing the duty of redemption for her son, Mahlon. Naomi was so involved in caring for the baby that the entire town recognized that the baby eased Naomi's grief over her son's deaths. The record says: "Then Naomi took the child, laid him in her lap and cared for him. The women living there said, 'Naomi has a son' " (Ruth 4:16, 17).

Ruth could easily have resented Naomi's intrusion, but because she loved Naomi, Ruth cheerfully shared the happiness of caring for her baby.

The Bible consistently presents the picture that the hand of God is over all, and that all that happens is with His knowledge and foreknowledge. For those who love God and put Him first, all things work together for their ultimate good (Romans 8:28). We see this illustrated in the lives of Boaz and Ruth, who not only demonstrated commitment to God but also put others' interests ahead of their own.

CHAPTER 8

Tender Love: Elkanah and Hannah

The Bible gives us a close-up view into the domestic life of a godly couple who lived toward the end of the period of the judges. The setting is the Feast of Tabernacles, a joyous celebration of freedom and thanksgiving. But we find the wife, Hannah, weeping and unable to eat because she is childless. Elkanah, her husband, loves her dearly and does all he can to comfort her.

Incidentally, Samuel himself could not have authored the book that bears his name and tells his story because a lot of the history covered by the book took place after his death. Yet the book acquired neither the name of David nor of Saul, the first two kings of Israel, but of Samuel, who anointed them both. Any list of the most important persons in the history of Israel must include Samuel. In him are combined the roles of ruler, prophet, and also priest.

Often children are identified by who their parents are. But sometimes, parents are known by who their children become. Elkanah and Hannah did nothing extraordinary, except raise Samuel. Their child appeared to be God-given because Hannah was barren so very long, but they are neither the first ones nor the last to acquire a child after a prolonged period of anxiety. Others, in beseeching God for a child, have also made great promises and fulfilled them. Most of these have gone unrecorded. But the

Tender Love: Elkanah and Hannah

remarkable child Samuel caused the memory of Elkanah and Hannah to be preserved.

Of the couples discussed in this book, most of the husbands were patriarchs, prophets, or rulers. We ourselves cannot become such people. But we can all be like Elkanah and Hannah. Our children may not become as famous as Samuel, but if we can show the same dedication as Elkanah and Hannah, perhaps we can bring the extraordinary out of the ordinary.

Elkanah is not the only ordinary man to become known because of Samuel's fame. The names of Jehoram, his father; Elihu, his grandfather; Tohu, his grandfather's father; and Zuph, his grandfather's grandfather; are also recorded. Of Zuph we know practically nothing, except that he must have been a significant enough person for his decendants to be called Zuphites (1 Samuel 1:1, 2).

Zuph is labeled an Ephraimite in Samuel's genealogy in 1 Samuel 1:1. But another genealogy in 1 Chronicles 6:33–38 lists Zuph and his descendants under the line of Kohath, son of Levi. Perhaps the label "Ephraimite" for Zuph indicates the area where he lived, rather than the name of his tribe. Several cities in the hill country of Ephraim were allotted to the Levites, including Shechem, the city of refuge (Joshua 21:20, 21). Also, at times, the entire northern kingdom of Israel was called Ephraim (Hosea 4:17; 5:3, 5, 9, 11, 13), just as the entire southern kingdom was called Judah.

Hannah's problem

Elkanah had two wives, Hannah and Peninnah. *Hannah* means "the graceful one," and *Peninnah* means "the fertile one." While their parents had no way of knowing the future, the names they chose turned out to be especially appropriate.

Polygamy among Israelites, while frequent among kings, was practiced among commoners by those whose first wife had produced no heirs. Hannah's problem is not only that she had no children, but that Peninnah had several.

Elkanah took his family to the tabernacle at Shiloh every year. All males were required to make the journey three times a year—the Feast of Unleavened Bread, the Feast of Pentecost, and the Feast of

Tabernacles. The most joyous of these was the Feast of Tabernacles. During this festival, Israelites lived in booths that reminded them of their journey through the wilderness. The festival was like a massive camp meeting and just as much fun. The feast was also a thanksgiving and followed the autumn harvests. Harvest celebrations in any culture are especially festive.

But despite the festivity, or maybe because of it, Hannah remained sorrowful especially because Peninnah chose these occasions to mock her barrenness. The Bible says this went on year after year. Peninnah would provoke Hannah till she wept and refused to eat (1 Samuel 1:6, 7).

Peninnah knew that Elkanah loved Hannah more. Peninnah perhaps had assumed that as the mother of Elkanah's firstborn, she would become the favored one. The Law of Moses also dictated that if a man had two wives and did not love one of them and both of them bore him sons, he had to give the son of the unloved wife a double portion of everything owned, if he were the firstborn (Deuteronomy 21:15–17).

Because Hannah continued as favorite wife, Peninnah made snide remarks about Hannah's inability to bear children and made life miserable for her. Wrong tactic. The gentle disposition of Hannah and her refusal to retaliate naturally drew Elkanah closer and closer to her, frustrating Peninnah further.

Elkanah's tenderness

Elkanah made the annual trip to Shiloh partly for the annual feast but also to offer a thank offering in fulfillment of some vow he had made earlier (1 Samuel 1:21). Elkanah took home his portion of the sacrifice[1] and, dividing the meat, gave a portion for Peninnah and for each of her children.

But he gave Hannah a double portion (1 Samuel 1:4, 5)—the same she would have received if she had a child. Of course it wasn't the same as having a child, but the thought that Elkanah was thoughtful and considerate counted for something. The Bible doesn't say Elkanah gave her the double portion because she didn't have any children or because he wanted to pretend she had one but because "he loved her" (1 Samuel 1:5).

Tender Love: Elkanah and Hannah

Also "Elkanah . . . would say to her, 'Hannah, why are you weeping? Why don't you eat? Why are you downhearted? Don't I mean more to you than ten sons?' " (1 Samuel 1:8). Though he said this kindly and tenderly, Hannah's heart must have wanted to shout, "I want a baby!" But, of course, she kept quiet except for her sobs because she knew he meant well.

Elkanah's attitude was patronizing, but it accompanied a genuine love for Hannah. Evidently, they enjoyed a special relationship. Elkanah believed that he meant a lot to Hannah. But he did not understand that having the best, most-loving husband in the world could not compensate for not having a child.

Taking it to God in prayer

As mentioned earlier, Hannah's greatest periods of sorrow occurred at Shiloh. The double portion Elkanah gave Hannah at that time increased Peninnah's jealousy, who took out her resentment on Hannah, taunting her till she cried. Fortunately, the sanctuary was conveniently near. Getting up from the meal she fled to the sanctuary, where she wept and poured out her heart to God, saying: " 'O LORD Almighty, if you will only look upon your servant's misery and remember me, and not forget your servant but give her a son, then I will give him to the LORD for all the days of his life' " (1 Samuel 1:11).

Eli, the high priest, sat on a chair by the entrance to the temple. He could not hear anything, for she was not praying aloud. He only saw her lips moving.

But everyone knew he could not even see properly. Note his progressive blindness:
1. The old, feeble priest has only heard about what everyone else has seen his wicked sons doing (1 Samuel 2:22–24).
2. When Samuel received his first vision, the Bible says that Eli's eyes were becoming so weak he could barely see (1 Samuel 3:2).
3. When a messenger came to report that the ark had been captured by the Philistines, Eli is recorded as having eyes that were "set so that he could not see" (1 Samuel 4:15).

The little Eli could see led him to believe that Hannah was drunk. But she explained that it was deep sorrow, anguish, and grief that had caused her to pour our her petition to the Lord. Without probing into her problem, the kind priest told her, " 'Go in peace, and may the God of Israel grant you what you have asked of him' " (1 Samuel 1:17). His words brought great consolation to Hannah. Her heart became lighter, and she was able to eat (1 Samuel 1:18).

Hannah vowed, first, that if God granted her wish and gave her a son, that she would give him back to the Lord and, second, that she would not cut his hair all his life. The significant part of her vow is that the dedication would be for the entire life of her son. A priest's service for the Lord lasted twenty-five years, from the age of twenty-five to fifty (Numbers 8:23, 24). A Nazirite's vow was usually for a limited period of time (Numbers 6:5, 13, 18). But Hannah's son was to be dedicated for life.

Within a short time of returning to their home in Ramah, Hannah became pregnant. When the boy was born, she named her son Samuel, which sounds like the Hebrew for "God heard." Hannah explained the reason for the name: "because I asked the Lord for him." She had asked; God had heard.

Elkanah's support for Hannah's vow

When Hannah vowed to dedicate her son as a Nazirite and to give him to the Lord's service, she did this without consulting her husband. Samuel was his son also, and he had a say in the boy's future. A few months later, when it became time to make the annual trip again to Shiloh, Hannah informed Elkanah that she would skip the pilgrimage that year and wait until she could take Samuel and leave him permanently at the tabernacle (1 Samuel 1:21, 22).

Women who made vows sometimes faced opposition in keeping them. So Moses presented detailed rules governing vows. A father could nullify the vows made by his single daughter. A newly married man could nullify the vow made by his wife before they were married, and a husband could nullify the vows made by his wife. But

Tender Love: Elkanah and Hannah

they had to nullify the vow the first time they heard of it (Numbers 30:3–15.).

If the husband didn't immediately nullify a woman's vow when he first heard of it, but waited until later, the wife would still be released from her vow, but the guilt of the broken vow would rest on the husband (Numbers 30:15).

The Bible does not tell us when Hannah announced her vow to Elkanah, but when she informed him of her desire to stay home until the boy was weaned, he did not object. He responded, "Do what seems best to you." Hannah would surely have felt warmed by her husband's support.

Fulfilling the vow

Hannah couldn't leave Samuel at the tabernacle till he was weaned. A passage in the apocrypha indicates that this could be as long as three years. That would have given her some time to enjoy her baby and give him basic training.

When Samuel was ready to be taken to the tabernacle, Hannah took a three-year-old bull,[2] an ephah of flour, and a skin of wine for a thank offering.[3] A three-year-old bull was very valuable. Normally a year-old animal was sacrificed. Grain offerings were also brought to God (Leviticus 2), part of which was sacrificed and part of which was given to the priests for their use.

Hannah expected Eli, with a little prompting, to remember the incident that had taken place several years earlier. At that time Eli had told her, without knowing her petition, "May the God of Israel grant you what you have asked." Hannah reminded him, "I prayed for this child, and the Lord has granted me what I asked of Him."

There might be a subtle play on the word *ask* here. The Hebrew words for *petition* and *ask* stem from the same root, which occurs seven times in this chapter. In the final verse of 1 Samuel 1, the KJV and the RSV use the word *lent* for Hannah's "giving" him to the Lord. The word is actually a passive participial form of *ask*. Literally, Samuel would be "asked for" for the Lord's work. Interestingly, the word for *asked for* is *saul*.

Hannah's prayer

Then Hannah prayed a beautiful prayer that she might have composed. If it had been composed by someone else, it applied to her situation very well. Some call this the Magnificat of the Old Testament. We may compare excerpts of her prayer of praise with that of Mary's Magnificat in the New Testament.

HANNAH (1 Samuel 2)

Opening praise
" 'My heart rejoices in the LORD [2:1];

Reason for praise
" 'in the LORD my horn
   is lifted high.
My mouth boasts over my
   enemies,
   for I delight in your
     deliverance [2:1].

Description of God
" 'There is no one holy like the
   LORD;
   there is no one besides you;
   there is no Rock like our God
     [2:2]. . . .

Antithesis
" 'The bows of the warriors are
   broken,
   but those who stumbled are
     armed with strength.
Those who were full hire
   themselves out for food,
   but those who were hungry
     hunger no more [2:4, 5].' "

MARY (Luke 1)

Opening praise
" 'My soul glorifies [*magnifies*]
   the LORD
   and my spirit rejoices in God
     my Savior [1:46, 47],

Reason for praise
" 'for he has been mindful
   of the humble state of his
     servant.
From now on all generations will
   call me blessed [1:48],

Description of God
" 'for the Mighty One has done
   great things for me—
   holy is his name [1:49]. . . .

Antithesis
" 'He has brought down rulers
   from their thrones
   but has lifted up the humble.
He has filled the hungry with
   good things
   but has sent the rich away
     empty' " [1:52, 53].

Tender Love: Elkanah and Hannah

Those who argue that Hannah is reciting a previously composed song point to some parts that don't exactly fit her situation. Verse 5 reads, " 'She who was barren has borne seven children,' " whereas Hannah gave birth only to three other sons and two daughters (1 Samuel 2:21). Also, the song refers to a "king," whereas it was Hannah's firstborn son, Samuel, who anointed the first king much later. So, at the time of Hannah's song there could have been no king over Israel.

But these are not serious difficulties. The mention of "seven children" in her song need not refer to the number of her children. Additional children were future to the song, and seven was perceived as the ideal number. Also, the "king" could have been a local ruler, or it could be in prophetic use as the song also refers to the "anointed," literally the Messiah.

The parts of the song that do apply personally to Hannah were rejoicing in the Lord because He delivered her from her enemies (2:1), persecution by a loud-mouthed arrogant person (2:3), and the one who was childless being barren no longer (2:5).

The song also contains a reference to Peninnah in the line " 'but she who has had many sons pines away' " (1 Samuel 2:5). Also, the " 'wicked [who] will be silenced in darkness' " (1 Samuel 2:9), are all those who have declared that the barrenness of Hannah was evidence of her wickedness. But now that she had a son, Hannah felt that God had vindicated her, and she was exuberant in her gratitude.

Yearly pilgrimages

When Samuel was to be given to the tabernacle, the record says, "*she* took the boy with her" (1 Samuel 1:24). Though not mentioned, Elkanah must have been present with Hannah because 1 Samuel 2:11 says that Elkanah went home to Ramah, but the boy ministered before the Lord. Though Hannah is the one not mentioned this time, they must have gone home together.

Together Hannah and Elkanah made the annual pilgrimage to Shiloh and used the opportunity to visit Samuel and to present him with a robe (1 Samuel 2:19). Peninnah is not mentioned again.

FOR BETTER OR FOR WORSE

The innocence of the young lad Samuel as he grew is heightened in the story by a foil—the wickedness of Eli's sons Hophni and Phinehas. The author of 1 Samuel contrasts the characters in alternating paragraphs in the remainder of chapter 2:

Eli's sons treat meat sacrifices with contempt (2:12–17).

          The boy Samuel ministers before the Lord. Parents visit (2:18–21).

Eli's failure to control his sons (2:22–25).

          Samuel's model development (2:26)

Prophecy against the house of Eli (2:27–36).

Hophni and Phinehas had a father who was practically blind and was unable to control them. Samuel had godly parents who visited him regularly. The role of parenting in the development of character is obvious in this passage.

During these annual visits to the sanctuary, Eli, the agent of God's blessing to Hannah, recited his blessings each year, saying, " 'May the LORD give you children by this woman to take the place of the one she prayed for and gave to the LORD' " (1 Samuel 2:20). God blessed Hannah with three sons and two daughters to replace the son she gave to the Lord.

Samuel's development as described in 1 Samuel 2:26 is strikingly similar to Jesus' development as described in Luke 2:52. Samuel grew in stature and in favor with the Lord and with men. Luke re-

Tender Love: Elkanah and Hannah

cords, "And Jesus grew in wisdom and stature, and in favor with God and men." Just as Jesus developed, we see Samuel growing physically, socially, and morally.

Elkanah and Hannah are not mentioned again. But the quiet, gentle woman, whose hurt God healed, and the husband who loved her so tenderly, had done their work well.

---

1. Only the fat and the inedible parts of sacrifices were burnt. In the case of sin offerings, the priests ate the meat. The bulk of the thank offering was returned to the worshiper, who shared it with his family. See Leviticus 7:16–19.

2. The KJV is probably mistaken in understanding that she brought three bulls (verse 24), especially since verse 25 refers to "a bullock."

3. A prescribed amount of flour and wine as an offering often accompanied a sacrifice of bulls, rams, and lambs (Numbers 28:11–15).

CHAPTER 9

Steadfast Love: The Jobs

Most wedding vows include faithfulness in sickness and health, prosperity and adversity, but few have experienced the extremes of these. Yes, even great prosperity can affect a person's faith and marriage. Many marriages have broken down with less prosperity or severe adversity than the Jobs endured.

Job is presented as a normative character. That is, only his good points are presented to better illustrate a point. He is described as perfect and upright even though he was a sinful human being like all the rest of us. God could call Job perfect and upright because he loved God supremely.[1]

Job's wife is presented as a satiric character. She speaks only once, when she tells Job, "Curse God and die." Presumably, she was a model wife in every other way, caring for her household, ministering to her suffering husband, taking food to him, nursing his boils, etc. But her positive acts are not recorded in order to highlight Job's trust by contrast. Job's wife endured the entire ordeal with him. She suffered the same losses he did—except the loss of health—perhaps more intensely. But she was loyal to her husband until the end.

Storywriters use the term *dramatic irony* to describe a situation in which the characters do not know something that is revealed only to the readers or audience. Denied this information, the characters grope as if blindfolded on a stage. In the story of Job, the curtains

Steadfast Love: The Jobs

are pulled back to reveal scenes in heaven. The readers are alerted to Satan's intentions to strike Job's property and health. But Job and his wife do not know this. Nor do the friends who come to visit him. More than anyone else, Job's wife was aware of her husband's character, which did not warrant such terrible suffering. Not knowing about Satan and his claims, she assumed the calamities had come from God. Knowing something sinister was going on, she blurted out to her stricken husband, "Curse God and die."

Both the Jobs suffered with their losses. But the way the wife responded is how Satan predicted Job would have—the same way most of us would have under those circumstances. The Bible says Job "did not sin with his lips" (Job 2:10, NKJV), which leaves the possibility that he had some questions in his heart.

The strong wisdom nature of the book of Job and the names of the characters in the story suggest an Edomite setting. The closest we can get to a name in the Bible similar to Job's is an Edomite king, Jobab (Genesis 36:34). Eliphaz, Uz, and Teman are also Edomite names. Shuah, on the other hand (Bildad was a Shuhite), was a son of Abraham through Keturah. The Bible has not recorded the name of Job's wife for us. However, a segment of Jewish tradition, based on a very flimsy connection, names her as Dinah, the daughter of Jacob. The connection is based upon the word for *foolish* used in both accounts. When Dinah's brothers heard what Shechem had done, they referred to the deed as "foolish" (Genesis 34:7). When Job's wife blurted out, "Curse God and die," Job reprimanded her saying she spoke as a foolish woman (Job 2:10).

The temporal setting of the story is the patriarchal period. The characters live as semi-nomads, and their wealth is measured in livestock. Job's life span (140 years after his recovery) is also comparable to the life span of Abraham (175 years), Isaac (188 years), and Jacob (147 years).

Faithful in prosperity

The Bible lists the riches of the Jobs as seven thousand sheep, three thousand camels, five hundred yoke of oxen, five hundred donkeys, and a large number of servants (Job 1:3). The numbers, sevens and threes, and fives and fives, add up to tens. This, together with the numbers hundreds and thousands, convey the idea of completeness of riches. Their wealth in animals is consistent with the economy of a semi-nomadic lifestyle. Abraham, Isaac, and Jacob measured their wealth in the same terms (Genesis 12:16; 13:2; 26:14; 30:43).

The sheep yielded food and wool, camels transported goods to distant markets, oxen plowed fields, and the female donkeys were used for breeding. Owning these livestock would be equivalent today to having several industries with a large work force, and a fleet of trucks and ships to transport goods all over the world. The Jobs would be among the richest families on earth.

Such wealth is not normally associated with spirituality. In stereotypes, saints are supposed to live in poverty or near poverty, and wealth does not normally promote a relationship with God. That is why Jesus said it is easier for a camel to go through the eye of a needle than for a rich man to enter the kingdom of heaven (Matthew 19:24).

Several temptations may be associated with riches. (1) Riches are normally accompanied by secularism. Wealthy people don't need to trust God for what they need. They can buy it. (2) Abundant earthly possessions can decrease the desire for heaven. The more people have on earth, the less they have to look forward to in heaven. (3) The desire for riches is addictive. No matter how much one has, one is seldom satisfied.

But the Jobs were both wealthy and righteous. Their riches had done nothing to affect their relationship to God. In fact, Job credited God with all his wealth (Job 1:21) and sacrificed liberally (one sacrifice for each child) each time their children completed a round of feasting (Job 1:5).

Loss of possessions

The losses suffered by the Jobs were totally unexpected. The setting for the disasters was normal life. The scene was pastoral. The oxen were plowing, and the donkeys were grazing. The children were feasting. Rarely do disasters give warning. If they did, people would prepare and minimize the effect.

Steadfast Love: The Jobs

Sabeans carried off the oxen and donkeys and killed the attending servants. Lightning killed the sheep and shepherds. Chaldeans carried off the camels and drivers. A wind knocked down the house where the children were partying and killed all of them (Job 1:13–19).

The blows rained in rapid succession like machine-gun fire. Before the Jobs could recover from one loss, "while [the messenger] was still speaking," Satan inflicted the next loss.

The destruction was total. Only a single servant was spared in each case—just sufficient to bring the report. A contemporary comparison of the Jobs' losses would be having one's business go bankrupt or losing one's job, having one's credit cancelled, one's entire possessions except the clothes one was wearing destroyed in a fire or flood, and all one's children killed in a crash—all in one day.

It seemed that both earthly and heavenly forces had joined together against the Jobs because trouble came from human marauders (Sabeans and Chaldeans) as well as from the sky (the lightning and the windstorm).

The disasters came from all four directions. Sabeans came from the south, Chaldeans from the north. Lightning came with a westerly storm, and the dreaded desert wind blew in from the east. There was nowhere to run.

The Septuagint[2] contains extrabiblical text that depicts the suffering of Job's wife after the losses. It describes the humiliation of selling her hair to buy bread. While we may view these statements as later additions, the picture of the Jobs reduced to poverty is absolutely correct.

Loss of children

The Jobs had seven sons, an ideal number. Three daughters brought the total of children to ten, a complete number. The feasts which the brothers held were possibly birthday celebrations. Whatever they were, the sisters were not left out. At the end of the cycle of feasts, probably a season or a year, Job would have his children purified, sacrificing for any sins they may have committed even if only in their hearts.

A cycle of feasts had just been completed, and a new round begun. They were back at the house of the eldest brother. Father Job had recently had them purified, and their sins, if any, sacrificed for. Yet, evil came upon them. A mighty wind caused the house to collapse, killing all of them (Job 1:18, 19). We accept the death of old people near the grave more easily than the death of young people. We mourn the death of good people more than the death of the wicked. Here we have the untimely death of ten apparently good children. Not one survived.

Eliphaz tried to explain to Job that God allowed only the guilty to perish. By inference Job was supposed to conclude that his children must have committed some serious sin, or that his own sacrifice for them was insufficient. " 'Who, being innocent, has ever perished? / Where were the upright ever destroyed?' " Eliphaz argued. He added, " 'Those who plow evil / and those who sow trouble reap it' " (Job 4:7, 8).

Bildad was less tactful. " 'When your children sinned against him,' " he lectured Job, " 'he gave them over to the penalty of their sin.' " He touched Job where it hurts most (the recent death of his children), to appeal to Job to repent of his sin (Job 8:4). The only comfort here is that Bildad assured Job that the children's tragic death was due to their own sin, and not to Job's.

At the end of the story, God restored Job's possessions twofold and gave him another set of seven sons and three daughters. No child can replace the loss of a previous child, but a new child can ease the pain of an earlier loss. Job's new sons and daughters replaced the old in perfect numbers. This serves to show that the restoration to Job, while not identical, was complete. This time around the Jobs got to see grandchildren and great-grandchildren (Job 42:16).

Loss of place in society

Job does not seem to have actually been a king. He said, " 'I dwelt *as* a king' " (Job 29:25, italics added). But Job was certainly looked up to as some sort of civic leader. The young moved aside when he approached, and the older men stood respectfully to their feet (Job 29:8). Job performed the functions of a judge at the city gate (Job 29:7–10). He was well respected because he was just. After

Steadfast Love: The Jobs

he had spoken, everybody kept quiet. The people drank in his words and beamed when he smiled at them (Job 29:22–24).

The activities of Job call to mind the husband of the ideal wife in Proverbs 31:10–31. He sat among the elders of the land at the city gate, where he was respected (Proverbs 31:23). The ideal wife meanwhile took care of the home and family (Proverbs 31:15, 22, 27), purchased fields and supervised the planting of vineyards, traded, and saw to charity (Proverbs 31:16, 18, 20). All of these could have been performed by Job's wife, too, while he sat at the city gate. Such a woman is praised at the city gate (Proverbs 31:31).

Suddenly the Jobs found themselves social outcasts. Friends, guests, and servants disappeared. Brothers and sisters abandoned them, only to appear out of the woodwork when his fortunes were restored (Job 19:13; 42:11).

Scholars do not agree on the exact translation of some of the terms. "Brothers" (Job 19:13) may be taken in either a literal or loose sense of the term. "My own brothers" is literally "children of my womb." This probably refers to his mother since his wife's children were already dead. However these terms are taken, it is clear that the ostracism was total.

People not only stopped honoring Job, worse, they avoided him. But those who should have left him alone, didn't. Little urchins who hung around for entertainment made fun of him (19:18), and irresponsible youth composed songs to mock him (Job 30:9). A few passersby stopped to spit on him (Job 17:6).

Animals often do this—step in to finish off a wounded fellow animal. When humans see a suffering person, they sometimes conclude that the person is cursed of God and therefore a candidate for torture. Job thus became the butt of their ridicule. Similarly, the crowd around Jesus, when He was arrested, grew increasingly bold, until they thought nothing of spitting in His face and slapping Him (Matthew 26:67).

A few people stayed by Jesus because they loved Him dearly, and their presence brought some comfort to Him. Job, too, had the comfort of at least one person, his wife. She hovered around bringing him food, ministering to his needs, tolerating his foul-smelling breath (Job 19:17).

FOR BETTER OR FOR WORSE

Loss of health

After the first round of trouble inflicted by Satan, the loss of all his material possessions and the death of all his children, Job responded by saying, " 'The LORD gave and the LORD has taken away' " (Job 1:21). In other words, he hadn't gone into the red yet. He had not lost more than what he had at birth.

However, after the loss of his health, that statement was no longer appropriate. He at least had had good health at birth. But now Job said, " 'Shall we accept good from God, and not trouble?' " (Job 2:10). A man once found an extra ten dollars in his paycheck and said nothing about it. The next time he found his paycheck to be ten dollars less than it should have been. When he complained, the payroll clerk asked him, "Why did you come only this time when it was less? Why didn't you come last month when you got extra?" To this the man replied, "I can tolerate one mistake, but two is too much!" Most of us take the good for granted but complain when evil comes.

The wisdom tradition of the day taught that a direct connection between sin and sickness existed. In fact, by observing a sickness, experts believed they could pinpoint the sin. This principle resulted from the premises that (1) God is in control of the universe, and (2) that God is just. It therefore followed that whatever happened in this world had either to be just or else it meant that God was either not in control or not fair. The tradition did not take into account the presence of Satan.

Job's actual sickness cannot be diagnosed. But these were the symptoms: His skin was broken and festering. Scabs had formed and maggots fed on his dead skin (Job 7:5). He was afflicted with frightening dreams and terrifying visions (Job 7:14). He had lost a shocking amount of weight (Job 17:7) and was reduced to skin and bones (Job 19:20). His breath smelled foul (Job 19:17). His skin turned black and peeled, and his body was wracked by a fever (Job 30:30).

It would have best suited Satan's purpose of getting Job to curse God if Job's disease could have been associated with some serious sin. Satan would also have selected an illness that would be expected to end in death. It was not just the physical suffer-

Steadfast Love: The Jobs

ing that bothered Job, but the moral implications. God had instructed Satan that Job's life could not be taken. But not knowing that, Job and his friends expected Job to die. As Job himself says, he had come as close to death as the skin of his teeth (Job 19:20).

Job's wife had held her peace up to this point. It is only when she saw Job suffering, groaning with this mysterious terrible disease, that she blurted out her feelings. More than anyone else, she knew that her husband was innocent and that something sinister was going on. Also, a woman often cares more for the health of her husband than the man himself does. Satan had asserted in the beginning that if God allowed him to touch Job's flesh and bones, he would surely curse God. Now Job's body was affected, and his wife—bone of his bones and flesh of his flesh (to use Adam's description of Eve)—cried, "Curse God and die." The loss of Job's health bothered his wife more than it did Job.

Prosperity and adversity

In the beginning of the story the Jobs were the ultimate picture of prosperity. Satan accused God of putting a hedge around them, their house, and everything they had. God had blessed their flocks and herds (Job 1:9, 10).

At the end of all the financial and personal reverses, when the Jobs were left with nothing but misery, having suffered disaster after disaster, and finding absolutely nothing to be thankful for, Job complained to God that he was hedged in (Job 3:23).

The hedge in chapter 1 is the same hedge in chapter 3. But Job and his wife had changed sides. On one side was prosperity and everything good. On the other side was adversity and everything evil. Satan's challenge to God was legitimate. "Anyone," he argued, "would support God as long as He continued blessing them."

In all sports, players alternately play from different sides of the net, court, or field. The sides are different, and one is often easier to score from. Some courts have a side that is terribly disadvantageous. The wind, sun, and bad surface might make it difficult or even impossible to score. Any player might win when the other has the bad side, but no one can be proclaimed a champion unless he can win from both ends. The Jobs had showed that they could win from the good end. When moved to the bad end, they showed that they could also win from that end.

※

Early rabbis noted similarities in the story of Adam and the story of Job. Both were outstanding men who faced tests of cosmic importance. The homes of both were specified to be in the "east." *Seven* was a significant number in both narratives. The wives of both appeared only later in the stories, and both were used as mouthpieces of Satan. One main difference is that whereas Adam listened to Eve, Job didn't go along with his wife's counsel.

But in response to his wife's cry to "curse God," Job did not call *her* foolish. He says she spoke *like* a foolish woman. She was not a foolish woman. This was not her normal behavior; this outburst was unbecoming of her usual conduct.

Job's wife must indeed have been his support during his ordeal. She must have suffered as she prepared his meals and bathed his sores. His gaunt body and peeling skin must have torn at her heart. She alone ventured close enough to get hit by his foul breath (Job 19:17). When she finally broke down, it was not against him, neither was it for her own sake, but for his. She had remained calm as asset after asset disappeared. She uttered no complaint when her ten children were felled in one blow. But the sight of her suffering husband was the last straw in the series of undeserved reverses. Hers was a righteous indignation. Job reprimanded her. But significantly, God had no condemnation for her at the end of the story when he condemned the others.

Adam and Eve had failed their test. The Jobs passed theirs.

---

1. For a fuller treatment of how God could count Job "perfect and upright," see Gordon Christo, "The Gospel According to Saint Job," *Adventist Review*, April 14, 2005, 10–12.

2. The Greek version of the Old Testament and apocrypha, most of which was translated in the third century B.C. It is called the Septuagint because, according to tradition, seventy elders did the translation.

CHAPTER

Selfish Love: David and Bathsheba

Adultery is a result of selfishness. The adulterer thinks only of pleasure and enjoyment for self. Nobody else counts, not even the partner. David's adultery showed that he cared for none but himself. He sacrificed a trusted guard and other innocent soldiers with him and showed disregard for another guard and an advisor. After his lust was gratified, he even sent Bathsheba home.

The adulterous incident also led to complicated, futile maneuvers to cover up his dastardly deed. These clumsy attempts ultimately threatened to consume David himself. In his affair, David broke the sixth commandment, "Thou shalt not kill"; the seventh commandment, "Thou shalt not commit adultery"; the ninth commandment, "Thou shalt not bear false witness against thy neighbor"; and the tenth commandment, "Thou shalt not covet."

Disregard for loyal associates

David's famous thirty heroes included three men famed for their daring exploits, along with an additional group of select warriors. The exploits of the thirty heroes are not detailed except for the daring activities of the bravest three. Second Samuel says there were thirty-seven of them but lists only twenty-nine, ending with Uriah. First Chronicles lists another sixteen after Uriah. Apparently, these are a total list of the group, who did not all serve at the same time.

New ones were conscripted, replacing those who died. Second Samuel 23:23 suggests that they functioned as David's bodyguard, but it is apparent that they also went to battle with or without the king. Obviously, the safety of the king lay in their hands. By necessity, some of them lived around the palace of the king.

One of them who lived near the palace was Uriah (2 Samuel 23:39). As a Hittite, he had a foreign origin, but that did not prevent David from drafting him into his most trusted band, which also included an Ammonite. When David sent messengers to inquire about the woman he saw bathing, and they reported that she was a married woman, wife of Uriah the Hittite, he should have dropped the matter immediately. David had plenty of choices from his harem. But he desired what he desired, no matter that she was married to one of his trusted bodyguards. If he was so unconcerned about a bodyguard, one of the elite thirty, what about ordinary citizens? Right then David was thinking only of himself.

Another of the famous thirty was Eliam (2 Samuel 23:34). Little is recorded about him other than that he was a son of Ahithophel. But the messengers also told David that the woman about whom he was enquiring was the daughter of Eliam (11:3). It takes some nerve to commit adultery with the daughter of a colleague, one who served him faithfully. But no, David was not concerned about the father, only the daughter.

The third man in the picture is Ahithophel, grandfather of Bathsheba. He had the reputation of giving advice as if from God. At least that's how David and Absalom regarded his counsel (2 Samuel 16:23). But David showed little respect for his most trusted advisor and his relatives. It is not surprising that later, when Absalom tried to usurp David's throne, Ahithophel joined the rebellion and advised Absalom to lie with David's concubines in the sight of all Israel (2 Samuel 16:22). What goes around comes around.

The men in Bathsheba's life—her husband Uriah, her father Eliam, her grandfather Ahithophel—were more than loyal citizens. They were trusted, faithful, high-ranking employees of the king; two of them were away from home on duty fighting the nation's enemy, not suspecting that their king was ruining their family.

Selfish Love: David and Bathsheba

No real concern for Bathsheba

David's actions show his lack of respect for women in general and Bathsheba in particular.

When David saw a beautiful woman bathing, he ought to have walked away from the sight. There was nothing wrong in having seen—he couldn't help it. Our sight is the greatest avenue for temptation. Temptation in itself is not wrong, but what we do with it determines whether we sin. Pornographic pictures may suddenly drop down while surfing the Internet, but men who respect women for who they are and not what they are will delete those pictures immediately. That is the easiest way to get rid of temptation.

David then sent messengers to find out about Bathsheba. That too may not have been wrong. Perhaps she was single and eligible to contract marriage. But the messengers brought back the message that she was married. David should have dropped the matter then and there, but he was not concerned about the woman's reputation as a married person.

David committed adultery with her and then let her go back home. The narrator of the story does not place any guilt on Bathsheba herself, but neither does he record any resistance on her part against the advances of David. There are several indications that Bathsheba was a willing partner. (1) The text does not say that the messengers had to bring her; it simply reports that she came. (2) There is no record of any protest. She does not appear to have screamed. The Law of Moses stated that if a married woman living in the city had sex with another man and didn't scream, she could not plead rape and should be stoned (Deuteronomy 22:23, 24). Perhaps Bathsheba was afraid of David's position as king. Many men have compromised their positions as rulers, teachers, and yes, even pastors, to snare a victim. Whether she was a willing accomplice or not, David showed no interest in getting her as a wife. He used her and sent her back home.

When Bathsheba reported that she was pregnant, David knew that the child was his. Yet he was not interested in marrying her, only in clearing himself of suspicion.

FOR BETTER OR FOR WORSE

Elimination of Uriah

First, David summoned Uriah from the battlefront and, after hearing a perfunctory report of how the war was going, instructed Uriah to go home. David hoped that Uriah would spend the night with his wife and cover up David's misdeed. David even sent a gift after him to put him in a good mood.

But Uriah considered it dishonorable to engage in such pleasures while Israel's army was at war. It seems that it was David's policy for soldiers to remain celibate while at war (1 Samuel 21:5). So it would then have been against policy for Uriah to spend the night with his wife and then return to the battle. The honorable Uriah refused to go home and slept at the palace entrance, refusing to enjoy conjugal and culinary pleasures while his fellows lived in tents and fought the enemy (2 Samuel 11:11).

Next, David tried to loosen Uriah's morals by getting him drunk. This has worked for countless people in countless situations, but it didn't work in Uriah's case.

If Uriah's sincere dedication to the country and the king pricked David's conscience, he didn't show it. To save his reputation, David decided to get rid of Uriah in the least suspicious way. He sent him back to the battle with a letter instructing the commander to position him where the fighting was fiercest and then to withdraw from Uriah, allowing the enemy to kill him (2 Samuel 11:14, 15).

The letter was probably sealed, or perhaps the hapless Uriah could not read. Unsuspecting, he carried his death warrant from his traitorous king to Joab, his executioner. The task was tricky. Joab needed to eliminate Uriah without endangering too many others.

The king gave no reasons for his orders, and Joab asked no questions. Joab was not interested in the king's motives, only that he be not criticized for sloppy execution. In addition to Uriah, several innocent soldiers were killed, and Joab prepared a lengthy explanation. He need not have worried. As long as Uriah was dead, David could breathe again. The king believed that his honor was intact.

Of course, David now had the option of not marrying Bathsheba, pretending he had done nothing and that the child was Uriah's. But with Uriah out of the way, he chose the option of taking Bathsheba as his wife.

Selfish Love: David and Bathsheba

David may have worried that word of his adultery might still leak out. Several people were aware: the messengers who first went to Bathsheba and the messenger Bathsheba sent with news of her pregnancy. And also the messenger who brought word of Uriah's death would be suspicious.

Readiness to sacrifice innocent soldiers

David had sent Uriah back to the war with a letter to Joab, instructing the commander to stage the battle in such a way as to ensure Uriah's death. This involved some complicated maneuvers, which condemned other brave warriors to unnecessary death. In his desperation to cover up his misdeed, David was prepared to sacrifice several innocent soldiers of his frontline squad.

Joab was concerned that David would become angry at the unnecessary death of soldiers who were alongside Uriah as they were sent on a suicidal mission. He anticipated that David would rebuke him for letting the men get so close to the wall. He imagined the examples David would cite for avoiding taking such risks. So he instructed the messenger to add at the end of the message that Uriah, too, was dead.

Joab worried for nothing. Relieved at the elimination of Uriah, David showed no remorse for sacrificing innocent lives unnecessarily and comforted Joab over the loss of the soldiers saying, " ' "Don't let this upset you; the sword devours one as well as another" ' " (2 Samuel 11:25). The king had the audacity to shift the blame to chance.

The shepherd and his sheep

After nine months had passed, Bathsheba bore a son. Nobody had said anything yet, and David could well have believed that everything was going to be fine. No doubt his conscience pricked him whenever he thought about it. While he appeared to have succeeded in preserving his honor, the fact is that he knew he had dishonored a woman, unjustly murdered her husband, and sacrificed other innocent lives in the bargain. What bothered him the most, though, was the thought that he had sinned against God (Psalm 51:4). The silence concerning the matter was too good to last. Just when he thought he would escape any negative consequences, Nathan the prophet appeared.

Nathan wisely spoke in a parable so as to keep David off guard and neutral. Nathan picked a theme close to David's heart. He told him of a poor man who had only one lamb that was like one of the family, eating with them and sleeping in his arms. David would have thought back to his childhood and lambs that he loved. When Nathan told him that a rich man who had many sheep of his own, took that beloved lamb from the poor man and had it cooked for his guest, David burned with anger.

Kings of the Ancient Near East and Egypt were often referred to as shepherds. A psalm of the nation describes God as taking David from tending sheep to be shepherd of his people, and goes on to say that David shepherded them with "integrity of heart" (Psalm 78:72).

Commentators have noted that when Samuel anointed Saul as king, he was hunting for his lost donkeys (1 Samuel 9:3), whereas when Samuel anointed David as king, he was looking after sheep securely in his care (1 Samuel 16:11). This difference suggested what the state of the nation would be like under them. Under Saul, Israel would be scattered. Under David, they would be secure.

David indeed had shown that he was prepared to sacrifice his life for his flock. When Saul attempted to discourage David from fighting Goliath, David reported that he had fought a lion and bear, killing them to save his flock (1 Samuel 17:33–36). Similarly, David was prepared to give his life fighting Goliath to save the country. It was these qualities that made him king material. But now David was sacrificing the country to save himself. Nathan had chosen the right parable.

The verdict

In his indignation David, as royal judge, pronounced two punishments for the person who killed and consumed the lamb of the poor man. (1) He needed to be put to death; and (2) he must pay back fourfold (2 Samuel 12:5, 6). David's reason for the sentence is " 'because he . . . had no pity.' " These are indeed interesting words for a person who had condemned innocent people to death.

Selfish Love: David and Bathsheba

Leviticus 20:10 commands death in situations of adultery with a married woman. However, this may not have actually been followed strictly.[1] For not screaming, Bathsheba, too, could have also been given the death penalty (Deuteronomy 22:24). It is not clear whether David is sentencing the "rich man" to death, or just pronouncing him worthy of death. There is little difference for the application. He had unwittingly pronounced himself guilty to the ultimate degree and worthy of death.

Of course this was now the right time for Nathan the prophet to tell the king that he was that condemned rich man. Uriah was the poor man. The sheep and cattle were all David's wives. The single lamb of the poor man was Bathsheba, his wife. Killing that one lamb was defiling that wife in adultery. The application was devastatingly clear.

The punishment

David had himself pronounced the verdict. Now God would give the sentence. The punishment as delivered by Nathan had three aspects:

1. " ' "The sword will never depart from your house" ' " (2 Samuel 12:10). This came true within a few years when his son Absalom killed another of David's sons, Amnon, for raping his sister (2 Samuel 13:28, 29). Later, Absalom himself was killed in a rebellion against David (2 Samuel 18:14). A third son, Adonijah, was later killed by the command of Solomon (1 Kings 2:24, 25).
2. " ' "[O]ne who is close to you . . . will lie with your wives in broad daylight" ' " (2 Samuel 12:11). This was fulfilled when Absalom his son, slept with David's concubines on the rooftop as he was advised by Ahithophel, Bathsheba's grandfather (2 Samuel 16:21, 22).
3. " '[T]he son born to you will die.' " The son who had just been born died (2 Samuel 12:14–19).

Repentance

After Nathan came to him, David composed Psalm 51 in genuine repentance. But the preceding Psalm 50, composed by Asaph, must have struck him often in the earlier days. The psalm condemned sacrifices made by people who stole, committed adultery, and spoke evil and pointed out that those sacrifices were meaningless (Psalm 50:16–23).

During the period before Nathan came to him, David had led a double life. He ruled the nation and pretended to protect the people's rights—but it was a farce. He worshiped God and took animals for sacrifice—but lived as a hypocrite. In Isaiah 1:13–15, God condemns the Israelites for bringing sacrifices that were meaningless because their hands were full of blood. This described a situation such as David's. In the core of his heart, a dirty deed begged for cleansing. But so long as nobody brought it up, he was happier to let it lie hidden than to bring it out in the open. Now that it was exposed, David could pour out his heart unhindered. He cried out,

> Have mercy on me, O God,
>   according to your unfailing love;
> according to your great compassion
>   blot out my transgressions.
> Wash away all my iniquity
>   and cleanse me from my sin (Psalm 51:1, 2).

The first step for David was to acknowledge his sin. This he did profusely. In the first five verses of Psalm 51, David uses the word *sin* and its synonyms twice in each verse. He does this again in verse 9. In response to the spirit of Psalm 50:8–15, 17, which condemned meaningless sacrifices, David continued, declaring that a broken and contrite spirit are more valuable than sacrifices. Once David's sin was brought out into the open, he could begin to heal.

David's second step was the desperate longing for the removal of his guilt, which had been gnawing inside him. Along with the acknowledgment of guilt are numerous pleas for cleansing. David uses the terms *wash away, cleanse,* and *blot out* several times (Psalm 51:2, 7, 9). God himself longs to turn scarlet sins into snowy white, but individuals must be willing (Isaiah 1:18, 19).

David prayed, "Create in me a pure heart, O God." It is not only the removal of uncleanness that he wants but a new heart and spirit

Selfish Love: David and Bathsheba

(Psalm 51:10). What appeared to have bothered David's conscience the most was the death of Uriah and perhaps the others with him. He cried out, "Save me from bloodguilt, O God" (Psalm 51:14).

Forgiveness

On two counts David was worthy of the sentence of death: First, for committing adultery with a married woman (Leviticus 20:10; Deuteronomy 22:22); and second, for having put an innocent man to death (Leviticus 24:17). In response to Nathan's parable, David had condemned himself to die. However, God recognized David's repentance as genuine and saw fit to forgive him. Thus Nathan informed David: " 'The Lord has taken away your sin. You are not going to die' " (2 Samuel 12:13).

Psalm 32 is one of David's most joyous psalms. In it David first describes his state after confession and forgiveness. The psalm begins:

> Blessed is he
>> whose transgressions are forgiven,
>> whose sins are covered
>
> Blessed is the man
>> whose sin the Lord does not count against him
>> and in whose spirit is no deceit (verses 1, 2).

At the end of the psalm David throws out this call:

> Rejoice in the Lord and be glad, all you righteous;
>> sing, all you who are upright in heart! (verse 11).

When Bathsheba's son died, as foretold by Nathan, David got up from the ground, washed, put on lotions, changed his clothes, and went to the temple to worship (2 Samuel 12:20). In time, Bathsheba bore David another son, whom they named Solomon. God was able to forgive David's sin and forget the crime to the extent that He was now willing to accept a son of David and Bathsheba. Nathan came back to the court to inform David that Solomon should be renamed Jedidiah, which means in Hebrew "loved by the Lord."

FOR BETTER OR FOR WORSE

Humans have not been as forgiving to David as God was. God declared, through Ahijah the prophet, that David had followed Him with all his heart, doing only what was right (1 Kings 14:8). First Kings 15:5 says pretty much the same thing but adds the qualification "except in the case of Uriah the Hittite." The passage condemns David, not for his adultery, but for the cold-blooded murder. But David repented even of that and was forgiven as evidenced by Psalm 32 and Psalm 51.

૭

The story of David and Bathsheba began when David as king, having skipped military duty, woke up from an afternoon siesta and strolled on his rooftop. There he gazed intently at a beautiful woman bathing while his army fought the enemy. This is a far cry from the one who challenged a bear and a lion to save his flock; who single-handedly took on Goliath; and who led his army to many famous victories. This idle David was easily snared by the devil.

The next time, David heeded the call of Joab his commander. He left Bathsheba with her newborn son, Solomon, and led his army against the Ammonites. He captured the city of Rabbah, took the crown from its king, and brought home great spoils and people to work as laborers (2 Samuel 12:26–31). He returned with the army to Jerusalem in triumph. The king had reformed his selfish ways and returned to selflessly leading the nation.

---

1. There was no thought to put Hosea's adulterous wife to death. The adulterous woman in the Gospel of John was brought to Jesus only to test Him (John 8:6). Jesus Himself released the woman with no condemnation, except to sin no more.

CHAPTER 11

Domineering Love: Ahab and Jezebel

Ahab's father, Omri, was one of the greatest kings of the northern kingdom. Long after the Omride dynasty ended, Canaanites still referred to Israel as the "House of Omri." He had extended the borders, subdued Israel's enemies, maintained friendship with Judah, and, like David, formed an alliance with Phoenicia. Similarly, just as David's son Solomon was married to a princess of Tyre, a marriage between Omri's eldest son, Ahab, and the princess Jezebel, daughter of King Ethbaal, sealed the treaty of friendship between Israel and Tyre. The marriage was a political strategy; the early part of Omri's reign was marked by the presence of rival kings Zimri and Tibni, and Omri needed all the alliances he could form.

The name *Ahab* literally means "brother of the father." He may have been so named because he resembled his father physically. Unfortunately, he emulated his father also in practicing evil. Many kings have been condemned for copying the sins of Jeroboam. Jeroboam, the first king of divided Israel, worried that his subjects would travel to Judah three times a year, as prescribed, to attend the temple feasts. To prevent this, he constructed two golden calves, established a new priesthood, and banned pilgrimage to Jerusalem.

What Jeroboam did was trivial compared to what Omri and Ahab did (1 Kings 16:31). Omri "sinned more than all those before him" (1 Kings 16:25), and Ahab broke even that record. Twice Ahab is mentioned as being worse than any of those before him (1 Kings 16:30, 33). Because none of the later kings of Israel or Judah equaled him in sinning and provoking God's anger, we could say that Ahab holds the all-time record for evil.

Ahab is condemned for specific evils (1 Kings 16:31–33):
1. He married Jezebel.
2. He began to serve Baal.
3. He set up an altar and temple for Baal.
4. He made an Asherah pole.

The ill-advised marriage with Jezebel led to the other three evils. While the alliance with Phoenicia brought military and trade advantages, it also brought Jezebel's demand to exercise her right to practice her religion just as Solomon's wives had done (1 Kings 11:1–6). To please her, Ahab constructed the temple to Baal and erected a pole for Asherah,[1] consort of Baal. Jezebel went much further—promoting the worship of the gods of Tyre and Sidon with the zeal of a fanatic missionary. The worship of these gods involved immoral practices that led to further apostasy in Israelite society.

The wedding

The Sons of Korah, members of the Levitical choir, composed Psalm 45 to be sung at royal weddings. The anthem was probably used at more than one royal wedding, but various phrases in the psalm have special application to Ahab and Jezebel, perhaps more so than to any other royal couple, with the possible exception of Solomon. Common elements between the king in Psalm 45 and Ahab as described in 1 Kings are as follows:

Psalm 45:8: palace adorned with ivory
1 Kings 22:39: palace inlaid with ivory
Psalm 45:12: Daughter of Tyre
1 Kings 16:31: Jezebel daughter of the king of Tyre

Ahab is the only king recorded as having lived in a palace inlaid with ivory. Solomon had his throne inlaid with ivory (1 Kings 10:18), but there is no record of another use of ivory in his palace.[2] Ahab is the only other king of Israel or Judah, besides Solomon, known to have married a princess of Tyre.

Domineering Love: Ahab and Jezebel

Psalm 45:10 calls for the queen bride to forget her people and her father's house. God had repeatedly warned the Israelites against marrying women from the pagan nations around them, fearing they would lead their husbands into idolatry (Exodus 34:16; Deuteronomy 7:1–3; Joshua 23:12, 13; Ezra 9:2; Nehemiah 13:23–27). Understandably, the Levitical choir exhorted the foreign bride to put away her past and to embrace the religion of the king.

This was applicable in the case of a foreign bride such as Jezebel. The singers had no way of knowing the devastating effect she would have on the nation in the future. Yet there was reason for concern. Sometime later, she set about systematically killing off the prophets of Yahweh (1 Kings 18:4).

The statement in Psalm 45:7 that says, "You love righteousness and hate wickedness" cannot be easily claimed for Ahab, but we must remember that quite possibly Ahab's wickedness began with his marriage and was therefore future to the wedding and this psalm, if it was composed then.

Jezebel's push to establish Baal worship

As queen, Jezebel held political clout. With religious fervor, she carried on in Israel the work of her father, king and priest of Baal and Astarte in Tyre. The temple of Baal, which Ahab built for Jezebel, doubtless included a "seminary" for the training of priests. Jezebel personally presided over the Baal cult in Israel and made it the state religion.

Jezebel showed her support for the priests of her cult by feeding 450 prophets of Baal and another 400 prophets of Asherah at her table (1 Kings 18:19). These experts in Baal worship were likely imported from Tyre. Eventually, Jezebel started killing off the Lord's prophets and would have eliminated them completely if Obadiah had not spirited away one hundred of them and hidden them in two caves, risking the ire of the wicked queen (1 Kings 18:4).

Elijah led the struggle to keep Yahweh worship alive. Appropriately, his name meant "My God is Yahweh." The religious conflict came to a head when Elijah burst into the presence of King Ahab and announced that there would be no dew or rain except at God's word (1 Kings 17:1). This was a direct attack on Baal—god of rain and, therefore, fertility.

Later, on the summit of Mount Carmel (in the absence of Jezebel, but in the presence of Ahab), Elijah exposed the impotence of Baal and demonstrated the power of Yahweh over rain. Ahab was as powerless as Baal. Helplessly, he watched the defeat of Baal and the slaughter of the hundreds of priests.

Back home that night, Ahab had to explain to Jezebel why she did not need to have food ready for all the priests the next day. When the king told her what Elijah had done and how he had exposed the impotence of Baal and then killed all the prophets with the sword, Jezebel plotted revenge. She sent a messenger to Elijah saying, " 'May the gods deal with me, be it ever so severely, if by this time tomorrow I do not make your life like that of one of them' " (1 Kings 19:1, 2).

The courage Elijah demonstrated on Mount Carmel vanished. From the high on the mountain Elijah descended physically and emotionally drained. Upon receiving the message from Jezebel, a curse formula for herself if she was unable to kill him by the next day, Elijah fled.

Jezebel was unable to keep her word, and the conflict between the worship of Baal and the worship of Jehovah continued. She sent for replacements for the slain prophets, and by the time Jehoshaphat came to visit Ahab, the wicked king was able to summon another four hundred false prophets (1 Kings 22:6).

Ahab's spinelessness

Ahab's marriage was arranged by his father. Many kings arranged marriages for their sons while they were still too young to choose their own. But Ahab showed that he had no resistance to Jezebel's wishes.

When she wanted 850 prophets imported from Tyre, he allowed it. When she desired to feed them from the royal kitchen, he gave in. When she started killing the prophets of God, he did not prevent it.

After the contest on Mount Carmel, Ahab had convincing proof of who the real God was. He explained the happenings in detail to

Domineering Love: Ahab and Jezebel

Jezebel, how Baal did not respond to the prayers of his priests and how Yahweh actually sent fire to consume Elijah's sacrifice. But Ahab was unable to convince her that Yahweh is the only true God.

Ahab was not totally opposed to God. Three times an unnamed prophet of God told him to lead the attack against the Syrians. Three times he obeyed (1 Kings 20:14, 15, 22, 28). But he failed to completely follow the prophet's instructions. When Ben-Hadad sent messengers to Ahab begging him to spare his life, Ahab easily relented and agreed to a treaty. A second prophet of God condemned Ahab's disobedience in sparing Ben-Hadad. The prophet delivered a prophecy of doom for Ahab (1 Kings 20:42, 43), who became sullen and angry.

Ahab invited the king of Judah to join him in battle. When the good king suggested they seek the counsel of God first, Ahab summoned his stable of about four hundred prophets who were trained to say what the king wanted. Only at the insistence of Jehoshaphat was a true prophet called. He foretold the death of Ahab. Then, before going into battle, Ahab requested the king of Judah to wear his royal robes while he went into battle in ordinary clothes to disguise himself. His fears were well founded, but his tactics proved unsuccessful. A stray arrow caught him (1 Kings 22:34).

Pushed by Jezebel

The Bible says, "There was never a man like Ahab, who sold himself to evil in the eyes of the LORD, urged on by Jezebel his wife" (1 Kings 21:25).

Besides importing her brand of Baal worship to Israel, Jezebel introduced another concept—the idea that the king could do anything he pleased, get anything he wanted by whatever means. Any obstacle in the way of satisfying a royal wish could be disposed of in any manner. Canaanite kings were despots, and Jezebel initiated Ahab into the only system she knew.

Ahab's father, Omri, had bought a hill from Shemer and built a new capital city for Israel called Samaria (1 Kings 16:23, 24). Ahab also ruled from Samaria (1 Kings 16:29), but he and Jezebel maintained a second palace in Jezreel. After the encounter on Mount Carmel, Elijah led Ahab back to Jezreel (1 Kings 18:46).

Next to the palace in Jezreel was the vineyard of Naboth, which Ahab thought would make a fine vegetable garden for the palace. Ahab offered Naboth two options: (1) a better vineyard somewhere else, or (2) full cash value. Naboth refused both offers. This was insulting to Ahab. His father Omri had bought an entire hill, and Ahab couldn't buy a vineyard. But Naboth refused not because he didn't want to cooperate but because according to the Law of Moses, family property had to remain in the family (Numbers 27:8–11).

Ahab became sullen and angry again (1 Kings 21:4), just as he had when the unnamed prophet had condemned him earlier for not killing Ben-Hadad (1 Kings 20:43). Only this time he also went to bed sulking and refusing to eat.

Jezebel couldn't believe Ahab's childish response to Naboth's refusal. She said, " 'Is this how you act as king over Israel?' " (1 Kings 21:7), which means, "Are you king or what!" This had the same effect as when wives demand of their husbands "Are you a man or what!" Or "Quit acting like a child!" Stung by such a remark, many men have been driven to do things they knew they should not do. Others have gotten themselves into deep trouble for succumbing to such pressure.

When Jezebel told Ahab to stop sulking and get out of bed, she coaxed him to "cheer up and eat," promising that she would get the vineyard for him. Ahab had no doubt she would. He must have suspected she would resort to foul means, but he did not have the courage to stop her.

Jezebel's advice to Ahab should be seen in the context of guidelines for Israelite kings. Samuel had warned the Israelites who begged for a king that kings would take their sons and daughters to be his servants. He would take from their produce to supply those who assisted him. Samuel warned that they would cry out for relief from the king (1 Samuel 8:11–18). When the Israelites still insisted on a king, Samuel wrote down regulations to govern kingship and prevent abuse of the people (1 Samuel 10:25). Before his death, Samuel reminded the people that none of them

Domineering Love: Ahab and Jezebel

could accuse him of misusing his power to cheat or oppress the people in any way (1 Samuel 12:2–5). They agreed the prophet had not.

Jezebel knew no such guidelines and adhered to no such regulations. She wrote out instructions in Ahab's name and used his seal and sent the message to the elders of the city. The Hebrew word for *elder* means "chin," or "beard," and implies that they were old enough to have a beard of considerable length. Elders had the kind of authority over a community similar to the way parents have authority over children. Because of the experience gained through age, they gave advice, bore witness, and served as judges.

Jezebel's instructions to the elders demonstrated knowledge of Israelite law. Naboth was to be accused of cursing God and king, and two witnesses were to be recruited (1 Kings 21:10). Mosaic Law demanded that anyone who blasphemed God should be put to death (Leviticus 24:16), and the minimum number of witnesses required for the death penalty was two (Deuteronomy 17:6).

Not only was Naboth killed, but his sons as well (2 Kings 9:26), which eliminated the problem of heirs laying claim to the vineyard. When Jezebel received the report, she then instructed Ahab to take possession of the coveted vineyard. It was as simple as that.

But the royal couple had flaunted all norms of decent government in the cold-blooded murder of Naboth and his sons and the confiscation of his property. In response, God sent his prophet Elijah back to Ahab with another prophecy.

For Ahab himself, Elijah prophesied that dogs would lick up his blood (1 Kings 21:19). This was not meant to be fulfilled literally. The expression, "Dogs will eat those belonging to Ahab who die in the city, and the birds of the air will feed on those who die in the country," simply means that not one would survive. All would perish wherever they may be. The predictions about Ahab's fate proved accurate. He instigated a war in an alliance with Jehoshaphat. Ahab was killed, and, though he was buried, dogs licked up his blood from the chariot as workers washed it in a pool in Samaria (1 Kings 22:34–38).

FOR BETTER OR FOR WORSE

For Jezebel, Elijah said that dogs would devour her by the walls of Jezreel. In her case, too, the prophecy was literally fulfilled (2 Kings 9:34–37). She was thrown from her palace window in Jezreel and dogs devoured her flesh.

Concerning Ahab's descendants, Elijah declared that every male descendant would be cut off (1 Kings 21:21). Sometime later, Elisha appointed Jehu to annihilate all descendants of Ahab (2 Kings 9:6–10). This order Jehu carried out scrupulously (2 Kings 10:11–14, 17). Jehu claimed to be fulfilling a part of Elijah's prophecy when he killed Joram, son of Ahab, and threw his body in the field that had belonged to Naboth (2 Kings 9:25, 26).

Surprisingly, Ahab meekly repented when he heard these prophecies. God accepted his repentance as genuine and postponed certain aspects of the prophecies (1 Kings 21:27–29). But they did not fail to be fulfilled. Ahab's repentance led to a period of peace.

But God did not forget what Jezebel had done. Centuries later, when the church in Thyatira harbored a woman who led others into immorality and idolatry, God called her a Jezebel (Revelation 2:20).

After Ahab's death, Jezebel continued to exert her evil influence on the affairs of Israel during the reigns of their two sons. The Bible says that Ahaziah, who reigned for only about a year, walked in the ways of his father and mother (1 Kings 22:52). Joram, his brother, was a little better. He did not do evil like his father and mother (2 Kings 3:2). He got rid of the sacred stone installed by Ahab, though it was installed again, probably by Jezebel. It was finally demolished by Jehu (2 Kings 10:26, 28).

Because Jezebel's daughter Athaliah married Jehoram, king of Judah, her influence spread over that kingdom too, especially during the reign of the other Ahaziah, son of Jehoram and possibly Athaliah. Athaliah coached her son Ahaziah in doing evil. He walked in the ways of Ahab his grandfather (2 Kings 8:27). After his death, Athaliah would have wiped out the line of David, but

Domineering Love: Ahab and Jezebel

baby Joash was rescued by his aunt Jehosheba, sister (possibly half sister) of Ahaziah, and wife of the high priest Jehoiada (2 Chronicles 22:11). Jezebel and her daughter, along with the kings they pressured, succeeded in ruining the kingdoms of Israel and Judah from within.

---

1. The "pole" has been translated "groves" in some versions. The exact meaning is uncertain. We may understand it as some sort of wooden representation of Asherah.

2. Almost a century later, the prophet Amos found it necessary to condemn the rich who owned summer and winter houses and who lived in houses adorned with ivory (Amos 3:15).

CHAPTER 12

Forgiving Love: Hosea and Gomer

Many believe that the story of Hosea and Gomer should not be taken literally. They doubt God would require anyone, least of all His prophet, to undergo such a tragic experience. Such people propose that the story should be understood as an allegory.

However, God has also used other prophets' family lives to illustrate their messages. Isaiah pointed out that he and his children were signs and symbols in Israel from God (Isaiah 8:18). Jeremiah was instructed not to marry or have children in order to reinforce his message of doom (Jeremiah 16:2–4). Ezekiel's wife was caused to die. God, who foretold it, instructed the prophet not to mourn for her (Ezekiel 24:16–18).

Thus we may take this story literally as the experience of a prophet who had a wife, lost her to other men, but lovingly took her back when she had nowhere else to go. This is not the only time such has happened. Throughout history, men and women have forgiven an unfaithful spouse and rebuilt a wholesome relationship. It is not easy, and it may take time to establish trust again, but it can be done if both partners are committed to saving the marriage and committed to doing God's will.

The prophet

Hosea's prophetic ministry spanned the reigns of Uzziah, Jotham, Ahaz, and Hezekiah, kings of Judah, and would have lasted approximately forty years. It is suggested that both Hosea's ministry and his marriage commenced about the same time. Nothing more is known about the prophet as a person. His father Beeri is mentioned nowhere elsewhere in the Bible.

Hosea's hometown is not identified. His messages were addressed to the northern kingdom of Israel, and he apparently resided there, the only literary prophet to do so. These were the closing years of Israel's history, but Hosea did not record the fall to Assyria in 722 B.C. He must have moved to Judah and/or written his book before that event.

Some have supposed that Hosea was in some way to blame for his wife's adultery. No doubt many times a person's adultery can be connected to some neglect by the spouse. Hosea's ministry may have occupied him considerably, but there is no evidence whatsoever that he failed in any way to fulfill his obligations at home. Hosea's faithfulness to his wife, Gomer, would illustrate the theme of God's faithfulness despite Israel's unfaithfulness.

Based on numerous allusions to baking in Hosea 7:4–8, some suspect that Hosea was a baker by profession. He uses phrases such as "burning like an oven" and "kneading of the dough till it rises." Hosea referred to the stirring of the fire; the smoldering fire at night; and the blazing fire in the morning. He compared Ephraim to "a flat cake not turned over."

The prostitute

The message of the book of Hosea opens with instruction from God telling him to marry a prostitute. "When the LORD began to speak through Hosea, the LORD said to him, 'Go, take to yourself an adulterous wife' " (Hosea 1:2).

The Law of Moses forbade priests from marrying prostitutes or divorcees (Leviticus 21:7), but Hosea is a prophet, not a priest. So the restrictions do not apply to him. While the NIV calls Gomer an adulteress, the Hebrew text does not call her a harlot, but uses the term "woman/wife of harlotry."

There are several options for how we may understand this:
1. She could have been the daughter or granddaughter of a harlot. Some female members of the families of prostitutes drift into the profession themselves later.

2. She could have been a flirtatious woman, whose public conduct with men went beyond social norms.
3. She may have been called a harlot by one with a prophetic knowledge of the future, just as Isaiah was able to say, "Babylon is fallen," years before it actually fell.
4. The book could have been written years later, by which time her character was fully known. A person writing many years after an event may refer to a person as King So-and-So, even though he may not have been king at the time of the events being written about but had later become king by the time of the writing.

Gomer was obviously a real person. The name *Gomer* has no significant meaning as do the names of the children she bore. She is referred to as the daughter of Diblaim, who also must have been a real person because that name has no significant meaning either. Furthermore, the value of Hosea's relationship with a real unfaithful wife has much more meaning than if the story were a mere allegory.

Gomer's unfaithfulness

Soon after Hosea married Gomer, we are told that she "bore him" a son (Hosea 1:3). The text indicates that Hosea was the father of the child. Gomer had two more children, but the text does not say that she bore them to Hosea, just that she "gave birth to a daughter" and "had another son" (Hosea 1:6, 8). This omission suggests that Hosea may not have been the father.

God instructed Hosea what to name the children. The first son was named *Jezreel*, which means "God scatters." The next child was a girl named *Lo-Ruhamah*, which means "not loved." Though God had supplied the names, it would be appropriate for Hosea to indicate he did not love a child that was not his. The final child was a son named *Lo-Ammi*, meaning "not my people." Again this could have been a sign that Hosea did not accept the child as his. In fact, Hosea declared, " 'I will not show my love to her children, / because they are the children of adultery' " (Hosea 2:4, 5).

Hosea reported that Gomer had given credit to her lovers for her food, water, wool and linen, and silver and gold (Hosea 2:5, 8). It is

Forgiving Love: Hosea and Gomer

preposterous to think that any person might not know who really was the breadwinner of the house, but there are several ways to understand and apply these passages.

We may take a cue from the attitude of the Israelites. They credited Baal, the god of rain and fertility, with the harvests of their fields and vineyards (grain and wine), wool, and oilseeds. They considered their gold and silver also as gifts from Baal and used these metals lavishly in the manufacture of images of Baal (Hosea 8:4; 13:2). Imagine God's reaction to their obeisance to Baal while He was providing rain for their crops, in addition to all their other blessings, including clothing and shelter.

An unfaithful person also may use food or money earned by the spouse for the home to support an illegitimate lover. When the spouse catches the cheating partner—in addition to the pain of betrayal—he or she may protest, "They're in my house." "They're using my car." "They're in my bed." Or, "They're eating my food!"

A certain blindness comes in with sin. This blindness clouds reasoning so that persons can come to such stupid conclusions as to excuse their actions. Gomer reasoned that her lovers supplying her with food, water, and clothes justified living with them. Gomer left home more and more frequently and for longer and longer periods of time till one day she finally seemed to have left permanently.

Recruiting the children

Hosea first attempted to recruit the children to his side. "Rebuke your mother," he instructed them. The children were surely aware that there was a problem in the home. The parents could not have hidden all the bickering, the questioning, the crying, and the frequent absences of their mother. The young children would have worried about what was happening and might have been grateful to talk about it. Hosea shared the problem with them but assumed their sympathy. "Talk some sense into Mom," he advised.

Then Hosea told the children that the marriage was over. Their mother did not care for him anymore and had another lover. "She is not my wife anymore and I am not her husband," he said sadly. He was still willing to make the marriage work, he informed them, but Mom had to reform. She had to quit what she was doing (Hosea 2:2).

Then he told the children that if their mother didn't change, he would take some drastic measures. Hosea threatened to strip their mother of her clothes and deny her food and water (Hosea 2:3). A husband was obligated to provide food, clothing, and marital rights to his wife. If he did not, his wife was free to leave the marriage (Exodus 21:10, 11). Hosea had done his part faithfully.

When a spouse is unfaithful, the natural instinct is to express anger, take revenge, and humiliate the guilty one to show how much pain the cheater has caused. In some societies today, a woman caught in adultery is stripped naked and paraded down the street to expose her lewdness. This is what Hosea threatened to do to Gomer in front of her lovers (Hosea 2:10). Hosea hoped this threat would help bring Gomer home and keep her there. Not surprisingly, the threat had no effect. Such emotional theatrics usually strengthen the errant spouse in his or her determination to leave.

Imprisoning the errant spouse

Gomer announced that she was going after her lovers. Much as he was angry, Hosea didn't want to let her go. He said,

> "Therefore I will block her path with thornbushes;
>   I will wall her in so that she cannot find her way.
> She will chase after her lovers but not catch them;
>   she will look for them but not find them" (Hosea 2:6, 7).

When we lived on a college campus, we knew several young people in love whose parents disapproved of their relationship. While it discouraged the couple, the opposition of the parents did little to stop them from meeting each other. Some of the couples planned to elope. Parents often contacted the college and instructed the hostel deans to keep the two from meeting each other. Some would say, "Lock her up till I come."

The natural instinct for preventing an unwanted relationship is to "protect" the family member with physical obstacles. Physically preventing the two from meeting may solve the immediate problem, but it does not prevent the affair from continuing. In fact, as many have realized, the "love" gets stronger in proportion to the opposition and the lovers become more determined to unite. Nevertheless, Hosea hoped that when his wife was frustrated in her attempt to contact her lovers, she would return to her husband, recognizing that she was better off with him (Hosea 2:7).

Wooing back an unfaithful spouse

After a series of threats Hosea finally declared,

"Therefore I am now going to allure her;
  I will lead her into the desert
  and speak tenderly to her" (Hosea 2:14).

This is a completely unexpected turn. Hosea has just condemned his wife, listed his accusations, and twice passed his verdict. (1) " '*Therefore* I will block her path' " (Hosea 2:6), and (2) " '*Therefore* I will take away my grain' " (verse 9). We are prepared for the third and final verdict, but it turns out to be a surprise. " '*Therefore* I am now going to allure her' "(verse 14). The Hebrew word for what Hosea is going to do means "romance or seduce." It is the tender way in which Shechem spoke to Dinah (Genesis 34:3), and the kind way Boaz spoke to Ruth (Ruth 2:13).

Hosea claimed that he would now lead her into the desert and woo her and speak tenderly to her (Hosea 2:14), he would give back vineyards (verse 15), he would betroth her in love and compassion (verse 19), and he would show love to her children (verse 23).

Earlier Hosea attempted to physically restrain his wife by placing obstacles in the way. Now he will try a different method, the same one that is used in the initial courting of a woman.

The story is told of a woman who went to her pastor to complain about her unfaithful husband. Deeply pained, she wanted desperately to take revenge on her husband and really hurt him. She informed her pastor that she wanted to divorce him. The pastor pointed out that her husband would not be hurt by it and might even be

FOR BETTER OR FOR WORSE

grateful for the divorce. She acknowledged that he might be right and asked how else she might really hurt him.

Wanting to help save the marriage but understanding human nature, the pastor gave the woman seemingly vengeful advice. He advised her to be nice to her husband and speak tenderly to him and make him fall in love with her again—and then hurt him. The woman agreed to try the pastor's suggestion. Weeks later she returned to the pastor to report that she had followed the pastor's advice, and it had been a complete success. She had stopped criticizing her husband and had talked affectionately with him, especially about the old days and the pleasant times. The couple began to spend more and more time together doing those things. Her husband soon stopped seeing the other woman and fell deeply in love with his wife again. The pastor replied, "Good, now divorce him. It will really hurt him." But, of course, the woman did not want to do that anymore because she had fallen in love with her husband too.

Hosea's first method of imprisoning his wife at home could be only a temporary solution. She was bound to escape sooner or later. Even if she didn't, there could be no real satisfaction in keeping her that way. But the second method had a greater chance for success. He had wooed her and won her once before, and he could do it again, provided he was sincere.

Certain elements in this passage compare to God and unfaithful Israel. The Exodus from Egypt and the worship of Baal (Hosea 2:15, 17) are relevant to the nation. But lest we start thinking that this narrative is an allegory of Israel, God gives Hosea another specific command: "Take her back."

Throughout his sad experience, though Hosea's attitude to his errant spouse had been punitive, he had never considered ending the marriage. He could have had her and her lover put to death, according to the Law of Moses (Leviticus 20:10; Deuteronomy 22:22), but a legal penalty is not always the best way to solve a problem. When finally Gomer had nowhere else to turn, Hosea could have felt smug. When she left home he could have been relieved that the quarrelling was over. But now the command of God came to forgive her, to love her again.

Forgiving Love: Hosea and Gomer

Hosea's faithfulness

God told Hosea, " 'Go, show your love to your wife again, though she is loved by another and is an adulteress. Love her as the LORD loves the Israelites, though they turn to other gods' " (Hosea 3:1). Note that Hosea is not only to take Gomer back, but he is to love her. Not just love her, but love her as God loves His people. The faithful prophet followed God's command again.

Where could he find her? There were several places to check, but she was not there anymore. Finally Hosea located her. But she was no longer the woman he had first courted. Her lifestyle had taken its toll on her health. By now, her lovers had abandoned her. She was now about to be sold into slavery. The menial tasks that she was now performing to support herself had further hurt her health and her spirit. Hosea found her on the auction block and bought her for fifteen shekels of silver and a measure of barley. A slave normally commanded a price of thirty shekels (Exodus 21:32), but either the barley made up for the difference, or else Gomer came at a discount, 50 percent off.

Forgiveness, while free, was not unconditional. Hosea instructed Gomer that she had to give up prostitution (Hosea 3:3). She had to stop seeing other men and had to stay at home.

Some believe that chapter 3 is but a second account of Hosea's marriage in chapter 1—that the woman and the incident are the same. The Hebrew word used here for *woman* is the word for *wife*. So, some argue, Gomer does not have to be already the wife of Hosea in chapter 3 but can be taken as a different version of how Hosea took Gomer, already a prostitute, in the first place. But significant differences exist between the two accounts.

1. The woman in chapter 3 is not named.
2. She underwent a period of celibacy, unlike Gomer, who bore children.
3. A price was paid for her, but no bride price was mentioned for Gomer.

The differences in the accounts are reasonable and easily explained. The woman is not named because we already know her name. The period of celibacy is a period of punishment or is necessary for purification. Gomer might have become a slave, and it may have been necessary to buy her back. She may have had debts that somebody had to pay.

Others conclude that chapter 3 speaks not only of a separate event, but that a different woman, a secondary wife, is involved.

There are strong arguments in favor of the theory that the woman in chapter 3 is Gomer, Hosea's wife, and that the incident is not a parallel account of chapter 1 but is a subsequent event. (1) God's command to Hosea is to love a woman/wife *again*. (2) Her return is anticipated in Hosea 2:7, where she said, " ' "I will go back to my husband as at first," ' " and by Hosea's attempt to win her back (Hosea 2:14–16).

Hosea, in taking back his adulterous wife, played to the historical situation. Such a dramatic portrayal was not necessary; he could have preached it through a parable. But his life story made such an impact on his hearers that the message that God loved His people Israel, even though they had been so unfaithful in running after pagan gods, came through clearly.

This was the message delivered by Hosea in words and in action: "To err is human; to forgive is divine." But if humans could forgive such great injury as Hosea forgave, how much more would God do so.

But the story contains more than spiritual lessons. The marriage of Hosea and Gomer is the best illustration of unfaithfulness and forgiveness in the Bible. They provide an example to show that any marriage, no matter how broken, can survive unfaithfulness and that love can be rebuilt.

CHAPTER

Jealous Love: Yahweh and Israel

Yahweh called Abraham out of Ur to Himself and promised him two things: (1) that He would make him a great nation, with descendants as numerous as the stars; and (2) that He would settle Abraham's descendants in the land of Canaan (Genesis 12:2, 3, 5, 7). In return, they were to worship only Yahweh (Genesis 12:8). God reiterated these promises on several occasions to Abraham, to Isaac, and to Jacob. We call this promise the Abrahamic covenant.

Centuries later, Yahweh identified Himself to Moses and informed him that He was about to fulfill those promises to Israel (Exodus 3:6–14; 6:6–8). God expressed the terms in the language of a marriage covenant between Himself and Israel. God promised to make them His people and to give them a land of their own to dwell in. In return, they were to be His people. At the outset of the Decalogue, God informed Israel that they should neither have any other gods, nor make idols for worship because, as He stated, "I the Lord your God am a jealous God."

The prophets considered the Exodus from Egypt and the journey through the desert like a honeymoon period. Not that Israel was loyal and did not follow other gods, but the Israelites had experienced a great deliverance in the Exodus and that event could be likened to the inauguration of the marriage promises (Hosea 2:15, 16; Jeremiah 2:2, 3).

FOR BETTER OR FOR WORSE

At Shechem, Joshua reviewed how the covenant had been first promised to Abraham, Isaac, and Jacob (Joshua 24:3, 4), how it was executed by Moses in the Exodus (verses 5–7), and how it had been completed by the driving out of the Canaanites (verses 8–12). Now the promises were finally fulfilled. God had given them their own land (verse 13). In response, Joshua instructed them to fear the Lord, serve Him, and throw away their foreign gods (verse 14).

The marriage sign

Circumcision was not a totally unheard of procedure when God commanded it of Abraham. The rite appears to have some connection with the marriage ceremony, as the word for *father-in-law* literally means "the circumciser." Scholars are not unanimous as to the reasons for the origin of circumcision. It may have been performed for physical reasons, such as to prevent disease in the wife. Whatever the reason, circumcision had value as a permanent sign that a man was married.

God took this marriage sign and gave it to Abraham with some modifications. Now the male was to be circumcised when he was an infant. This signified that the relationship began during infancy itself. Circumcision represented an initiation into the covenant community. God said, " 'You are to undergo circumcision, and it will be the sign of the covenant between me and you' " (Genesis 17:11). Even today, the ceremony of circumcision is referred to by Jews as the *berith* (covenant).

As the Israelites prepared to leave Egypt, the first set of instructions they received from God dealt with circumcision. Only circumcised males could partake of the Passover. Moses and Aaron followed God's instructions scrupulously, and only then were the Israelites brought out of Egypt (Exodus 12:48–51)

But like all marriage symbols—rings, necklaces, paint on the body, etc.—circumcision is only an external sign. Married persons may wear rings but by their behavior proclaim that they are still "available." On the other hand, one may choose not to wear a marriage sign, but still declare by conduct that he or she is married and not available. The more important thing was that the Israelites were

Jealous Love: Yahweh and Israel

to love God with all their heart and soul (Deuteronomy 10:12, 13). Moses went on to imply that this was circumcision of their hearts (verse 16).

Moses talked to the Israelites about the love of God, and then he urged them to put off their stubbornness and to respond to God's love. Mere physical circumcision did not guarantee that one belonged to God. There had to be a response from the heart. Also, just as physical defilement might be prevented by physical circumcision, circumcision of the heart meant that the heart had to be expunged of stubbornness, evil, and any other obstacle between God and His people.

Jeremiah described circumcision of the heart in terms of the putting away of idols. He declared that those circumcised only in the flesh—Egyptians, Edomites, Ammonites, Moabites, and yes, even Israelites—and not in the heart, would experience the fire of God's wrath (Jeremiah 4:1–4).

Though Paul referred to Abraham's circumcision as a "seal of the righteousness that he had by faith" (Romans 4:11), he goes on to say that Abraham is father not only of the circumcised but also of the uncircumcised who also believe. He pointed out that Abraham had not yet been circumcised when he first demonstrated his faith in God (verse 12). Therefore it is not necessary to be circumcised to be saved. That was the sign between God and Abraham's literal seed. Gentile Christians are Abraham's seed by faith.

Israel's unfaithfulness

The earliest Bible writers described Israel's lapses into idolatry as playing the harlot (Numbers 25:1; Judges 2:17; 8:33). Later prophets declared, " 'like a woman unfaithful to her husband, / so you have been unfaithful to me, O house of Israel,' declares the LORD" (Jeremiah 3:20).

The reigns of David and Solomon were characterized by general loyalty to Yahweh. But Jeroboam, the first king of the northern kingdom of Israel, changed that picture drastically. He was afraid that his subjects, if they made the journey to the temple three times a year, as commanded by Moses, would be tempted to defect to Judah. So he had two golden calves installed, one at Dan and the other at Bethel (1 Kings 12:28–30) and instituted a new priesthood. The Levites from all the districts of his kingdom responded by migrating to Judah (2 Chronicles 11:13–16). Later kings who led Israel to worship idols were likened to Jeroboam I (1 Kings 16:7, 26).

The later prophets condemned Israel and Judah for exchanging their glory for worthless idols (Hosea 4:7; Jeremiah 2:11) and for resorting to seeking help from other nations, instead of relying on Yahweh (Jeremiah 2:18, 19). Jeremiah charged that Judah's abandoning its trust in Yahweh was like forgetting her marriage to Yahweh. He put it in terms of a bride forgetting her wedding jewelry and ornaments (verse 32).

The prophets also described Israel's running after other gods with an embarrassing caricature, a female donkey in heat. Hosea described Israel as a "wild donkey" wandering alone (Hosea 8:9). Jeremiah went further, adding that male donkeys needed not to tire themselves pursuing her. She would find them (Jeremiah 2:24). In other words, no evangelism was necessary to woo Israel and Judah to heathenism. They themselves went seeking other gods. Other nations needed not to try and enlist their support. They got it voluntarily. Ezekiel declared that though most prostitutes charged a fee, Judah was prepared to make a payment for providing her own services (Ezekiel 16:34).

The prophets were incredulous over the behavior of God's people. Idols were merely manufactured goods. The woodsman, the carpenter, and the metalsmith created images that were like a scarecrow in a melon patch, which could not walk or talk (Jeremiah 10:3–5). They could not bring rain (14:22). The Israelites prayed to Baal, the god of fertility, for children. When they did have children, they credited Baal with those blessings. Hosea referred to these as illegitimate children of Israel (Hosea 5:7). The Israelites also credited Baal with their rain, their harvests, and their material wealth (2:8).

God's jealous love

The Old Testament consistently portrays God as a jealous God. Some versions use the word *zealous* in some passages, especially

Jealous Love: Yahweh and Israel

when it describes God's intense love for Israel, which makes Him angry with their enemies.

About idols, the Decalogue commanded: " 'You shall not bow down to them, or worship them; for I, the Lord your God, am a jealous God, punishing the children for the sin of the fathers to the third and fourth generation' " (Exodus 20:5; Deuteronomy 5:9).

Moses gave further instructions to the Israelites, telling them what to do with the local objects of worship when they entered the Promised Land: " 'Break down their altars, smash their sacred stones, and cut down their Asherah poles. Do not worship any other god, for the Lord, whose name is Jealous, is a jealous God' " (Exodus 34:13, 14).

But the Israelites forgot. Soon after the golden era of David and Solomon, Jeroboam installed the golden calves and the new priesthood. He also instituted new festivals in the northern kingdom (1 Kings 12:31, 32). In the south, at the same time, Rehoboam also led the people of Judah in setting up high places, sacred stones, and Asherah poles. "By the sins they committed they stirred up [God's] jealous anger more than their fathers had done" (14:22).

The punishment

God's jealous anger caused Him to sentence idolatrous Israel to the punishment of women who committed adultery. He declared, " ' "I will bring upon you the blood vengeance of my wrath and jealous anger. Then I will hand you over to your lovers, and they will tear down your mounds and destroy your lofty shrines" ' " (Ezekiel 16:38, 39).

The punishment befitted the crime. In the Abrahamic covenant, God had contracted to give the descendants of Abraham a land of their own. Living in the land of promise hinged on their loyalty to Yahweh. When they forsook him in favor of other gods, Yahweh was under no obligation to keep protecting them from the armies of other nations. Jeremiah's message from Yahweh was, " ' "As you have forsaken me and served foreign gods in your own land, so now you will serve foreigners in a land not your own" ' " (Jeremiah 5:19). Hosea named Assyria as the foe that would take Israel captive (Hosea 10:6).

FOR BETTER OR FOR WORSE

A hundred years later, Jeremiah prepared Judah for its own captivity. Jeremiah gradually unfolded the nature of the nation that would take them captive. First, Jeremiah told them the army would come from the north (Jeremiah 4:6). Then he informed them that the enemy would come from a distant land (verse 16). The next clue was that the enemy was from an ancient and enduring nation (5:15). The next hint should have brought anyone quite close to the answer. The nation to take them captive would not speak a language they could follow, but which would be very different (verse 15b). Finally Jeremiah named the country. God's punishment would come through Babylon (20:4).[1] Judah did not learn a lesson from seeing Israel unfaithful and were removed from the land that God had given them.

By allowing Israel and Judah to be taken captive and exiled from the land that had been covenanted to them, God was, in effect, "divorcing" them. Yahweh declared through Jeremiah, " 'I gave faithless Israel her certificate of divorce and sent her away because of her adulteries.' " God thought that Judah would have learned from Israel's failure and punishment but had to concede, " 'her unfaithful sister Judah had no fear; she also went out and committed adultery' " (3:8).

Jealousy for Israel

All love is jealous. One who truly loves another cannot bear to let him or her go. Some say, "If you truly love her, you will let her do what will make her the most happy, even if it means letting her go." Yet, genuine love cannot let go but hangs on and on till there is nothing more that can be done.

God's jealousy demonstrated the intensity of His love for Israel. When they had been taken into captivity, God's jealous anger turned against the nations (Ezekiel 36:5, 6). Some versions render the word *zealous*, when it is used in favor of Israel. This is the positive aspect of the same word. As the seventy years of exile came to a close, the Lord spoke kind and comforting words, declaring, " ' "I am very jealous for Jerusalem and Zion" ' " (Zechariah 1:13, 14). In fact, He said, " 'I am burning with jealousy for her' " (8:2).

Jealous Love: Yahweh and Israel

The restoration

However, with the punishment came a ray of hope. Earlier, Jeremiah had declared that the sounds of joy and gladness and the voices of the bride and bridegroom would be silenced (Jeremiah 7:34; 16:9; 25:10). Later, he added that the period of silence would be limited. Once more the sound of brides and bridegrooms would be heard in the land (33:11). He added the detail that the period of silence would be limited to seventy years. Then their oppressors would be overthrown (25:12).

Hosea referred to a period of time for Israel when there would be no pregnancy or conception (Hosea 9:11), but he added that after this would come a time of healing and love (14:4). So God's action was not really punishment, but discipline.

The prophets urged Israel to return to Yahweh, promising that He would be faithful in accepting them back. Though they were confident that Israel would return, yet they maintained that the restoration of the relationship could rest only on one condition—that God's people in returning to Him should abandon their idolatrous ways and rely completely on Yahweh again.

In fact this is exactly what Hosea recommended. He instructed Israel to ask forgiveness:,

> Say to him:
>   "Forgive all our sins
> and receive us graciously, . . .
> We will never again say 'Our gods'
>   to what our own hands have made" (Hosea 14:2, 3).

Yahweh promised that He would make an atonement for all that Israel had done (Ezekiel 16:63), but at the same time Israel and Yahweh both remembered that Israel was not able to keep the terms of the former covenant. While He was their Husband, they had broken the former covenant. So He changed things to make it possible for them. Now He promised to write the law in their hearts, to impress it on their minds (Jeremiah 31:33). This is the foundation of the gospel, the mystery of grace. This is the new covenant.

FOR BETTER OR FOR WORSE

God declared anew that Israel would be His people and He would be their God. But now He would give them singleness of heart and action so they would always love Him. He would inspire them to love Him so much that they would never turn away again. This is the everlasting covenant He would make with them (32:38–40).

Ezekiel's final chapters present a model constitution for restored Israel. He anticipated that God's glory would return to the rebuilt temple (Ezekiel 43), and a stream would flow from the temple, growing larger and larger into a mighty river, which would provide blessings for the entire world (47:1–12). Jeremiah records the following response to the thought of the new covenant and its restoration:

> " ' "Give thanks to the LORD Almighty,
>   for the LORD is good;
>   his love endures forever" ' " (Jeremiah 33:11).

---

1. Though the nation that took them captive was actually to the east, the Babylonians had to approach Canaan from the north, above the Sea of Galilee. Thus they are termed the distant north. They were considered an ancient nation, and their language could not be easily understood.